Ironman Lake Placid
Racing Tips and Strategies

Other Books by Raymond Britt

Racing Ironman: From Debut to Kona and Beyond

Racing Ironman Wisconsin

Qualifying for Kona

Chicago Marathon

Boston Marathon

Ironman Lake Placid:
Racing Tips and Strategies

By Raymond Britt

ISBN 1450569102
EAN-13 978-1450569101

Fourth Printing

10256007031001020304050607080809

1 2 3 4 5 6 7 8 9 10 9 8 7 6 5 4 3 2 1 000

Published by RunTriMedia Publishing

Chicago IL, Scottsdale AZ, Boston MA

Printed in the United States of America

Visit us at www.RunTriMedia.com.

For Wendy, Amanda, Rebecca, Eric and Kirsten

Contents

Introduction

The Destination

- What to Expect at Ironman Lake Placid
- Details, Entry, Schedule. Athletes, Kona, etc.

Racing Ironman Lake Placid

- 2002: Kona Slot #1
- 2003: Downpours and Crosswinds
- 2004: Ironman PR
- 2005: Silver Ironman
- 2007: The Easy Ironman

Bike Course Tips: Riding a 5:36 Split

IM LP Preparation and Racing Strategies

- Training Plan and Strategy for 2002
- Detailed Day-by-Day Training Plan 2002
- Everything You Need to Know

Finish Line

Acknowledgments

My invaluable team of training, racing and supporting partners have included Steve Abbey, Art Hutchinson, Joe Foster, Michael McCormack, Bob Mina, Barry Schliesmann, Michael Schiff, Kris Schriesheim, Rob Docherty, Kathy Winkler, Lisa Smith-Batchen, Michael Fisch, Marc Roy at SportStats Timing, Vinu Malik at xtri.com, Jesse Williams and Steve DeKoker at Brooks Sports, Adam Greene at Scott Bikes, Tim Moxey at Nuun, Rob Sleamaker at VasaTrainer, Jeff Banowetz at Competitor Magazine, and many more. I thank you one and all for the exceptional experiences we've shared so far.

Among many others, my Mother, Father, Wendy, Amanda, Rebecca, Eric and Kirsten have encouraged, inspired, shared and celebrated the journey with me from the beginning. This book is dedicated to them with unending love and thanks.

Author's Ironman Triathlon History

Race	Year	Swim	Tr1	Bike	Tr2	Run	Total
Vineman Ironman	1997	1:01:20	06:47	6:18:00	06:25	4:01:34	11:34:06
Ironman Canada	1997	1:14:55	06:30	6:15:55	05:20	4:05:01	11:47:40
Ironman Switzerland	1998	1:14:36	03:59	7:06:22	04:44	4:16:26	12:46:07
Ironman Europe	1998	1:12:08	04:33	6:17:36	04:04	4:02:10	11:40:31
Ironman Canada	1998	1:11:41	06:20	6:22:05	05:40	4:55:42	12:41:27
Ironman New Zealand	1999	1:11:32	07:45	6:23:00	06:40	4:19:07	12:08:04
Ironman Lake Placid	**1999**	**1:19:15**	**08:28**	**6:34:49**	**03:05**	**4:17:04**	**12:22:38**
Ironman Canada	1999	1:16:17	05:47	6:22:41	03:55	4:10:57	11:59:36
Ironman Florida	1999	1:18:43	06:43	5:35:01	02:52	4:12:38	11:15:57
Ironman California	2000	1:44:53	11:32	6:51:40	08:38	4:38:42	13:35:23
Ironman Florida	2000	1:17:01	06:55	5:44:39	03:21	3:57:46	11:09:40
Ironman Austria	2001	1:08:38	04:22	5:56:52	03:25	4:13:38	11:26:55
Ironman Florida	2001	1:10:35	05:33	5:35:07	02:18	3:46:42	10:40:13
Ironman Lake Placid	**2002**	**1:10:46**	**05:31**	**5:41:37**	**02:13**	**3:33:46**	**10:33:51**
Ironman Wisconsin	2002	1:15:29	08:41	5:37:59	04:25	3:36:17	10:42:49
Ironman Kona WC*	2002	1:18:57	04:01	6:01:54	02:15	3:50:14	11:17:21
Ironman New Zealand	2002	1:09:42	03:45	5:46:40	02:33	3:39:18	10:41:58
Ironman Lake Placid	**2003**	**1:12:19**	**06:42**	**5:50:34**	**02:12**	**3:37:21**	**10:49:06**
Ironman Wisconsin	2003	1:08:54	06:00	5:32:10	02:07	3:48:47	10:38:24
Ironman Kona WC*	2003	1:17:12	06:28	5:43:58	02:16	3:46:58	10:55:27
Ironman Lake Placid	**2004**	**1:11:56**	**06:35**	**5:25:18**	**01:59**	**3:26:36**	**10:12:22**
Ironman Wisconsin	2004	1:09:38	06:00	5:25:08	02:10	4:09:37	10:52:30
Ironman Kona WC*	2004	1:18:46	05:04	6:15:45	05:16	4:06:20	11:51:08
Ironman Arizona	2005	1:16:27	05:44	5:29:10	01:45	3:43:02	10:36:05
Ironman Lake Placid	**2005**	**1:11:41**	**07:18**	**5:37:10**	**02:42**	**3:43:10**	**10:41:59**
Ironman Wisconsin	2005	1:14:12	06:51	5:42:08	02:09	4:33:33	11:38:51
Ironman Arizona	2006	1:17:17	06:05	5:35:23	03:14	4:48:14	11:50:11
Ironman Lake Placid	**2007**	**1:19:17**	**08:37**	**5:50:53**	**04:27**	**4:07:06**	**11:30:18**
Ironman Wisconsin	2007	1:28:37	10:09	5:54:36	05:26	4:14:08	11:52:55

* Ironman Triathlon World Championship

Introduction

Lake Placid, upstate New York: the place where dreams come true for elite athletes for nearly 75 years. Host of the Winter Olympics in 1936 and 1980, the proud town has witnessed the epic, the unexpected and the truly remarkable, from Eric Heiden's world record gold medal performances to the USA hockey team's storybook gold medal victory in 1980.

In 1999, Lake Placid was chosen as the first North American venue for Ironman Triathlon. The challenging terrain, the beautiful landscapes, the inviting communities and the continuing support for exceptional athletics made Lake Placid, and its surrounding Adirondack towns, the perfect location for a new Race.

I immediately signed up for the inaugural Ironman USA, as it was known at the time. After competing in Ironman Canada twice, I looked forward to racing on the Lake Placid course, one that was billed as equally challenging, if not tougher.

The first Ironman USA took place on August 14, 1999, and it was a smashing success for the organizers and the town. The race smacked me more than I expected however, and I struggled to a 12:22 finish. The difficult course hurt me, but it also opened my eyes to one of the more spectacular events in the Ironman Triathlon series. The swim in Mirror Lake is exceptional, if not quite overcrowded. The scenic bike course is challenging but fair, and gorgeous. The run, taking place at the foot of the US Olympic ski jump training ramps, is also without compare.

It was clear after that first race in 1999: I would return to compete again. And I did. Of the 29 Ironman Triathlons I completed between 1997 and 2007, Lake Placid has been my favorite.

I've completed six Ironman Lake Placid races – 1999, 2002, 2003, 2004, 2005, and 2007. Each race brought different performances, different conditions, different outcomes, and different lessons. During those years, I qualified for Kona twice, but also struggled to finish. I had excellent days, and difficult ones.

The experiences are all presented here.

The first section features What to Expect on the Ironman Lake Placid Course, serving as a general race overview, and Race Details to outline key information you need to know: dates, athletes, schedules, contacts, Kona slots, etc.

The next five chapters detail my experience and perspectives from each race beginning with my return to Lake Placid in 2002, to earn my first Kona qualifying slot. Revenge of sorts on the course for the bruises of 1999, but also a celebration of the wonder of the race and the course.

After presenting a complete view of what it's like to compete, battle, overcome and succeed in Lake Placid, the book turns to the companion section: IMLP Training and Racing Strategies.

The first two chapters deconstruct the training plans and strategies I followed on my path to solid results at Lake Placid in 2002. Want to understand how you might train to race sub-11 hours in Lake Placid? It's all there.

The section concludes with Everything You Need to Know to Finish an Ironman, resulted from answers I've given hundreds of athletes over time regarding what to do before and during the race, relative to all the details. It assumes you've done the training, and focuses on everything else you might need to know, from nutrition to bike setup, from transition to finish. I follow these tips to the letter, especially in Lake Placid, and they can make the difference between good and great racing.

To bring the narrative and the racing experience to life, the book is illustrated extensively with photos that were taken by me before, during and after various Ironman Lake Placid races in 2005 and 2007.

Ready to experience Ironman USA Lake Placid? Buckle up, it's quite a ride.

Note: the race reports and racing strategies were written in real-time, that is, shortly after the events themselves, in sort of a diary format. I have not changed references to things like 'last year', which in context would mean the year previous to the race being discussed, for example, to preserve continuity and tone throughout.

The Destination

What to Expect at Ironman Lake Placid

Details, Entry, Schedule. Athletes, Kona Slots, etc.

What to Expect at Ironman Lake Placid

Each July more than 2300 triathletes will participate in Ironman USA Lake Placid. It's one of the more beautiful courses on the Ironman circuit, and can also be one of the trickiest.

With a tight swimming venue, challenging elevation swings on the bike course, and a tough run course, racers will be pushed to their limits. I've raced Lake Placid six times (1999, 2002, 2003, 2004, 2005 and 2007), and I can tell you: when you finish this race, you'll have much to be proud of.

For those competing in their first Lake Placid Ironman, and even as a refresher for those returning, here's what you can expect on race day.

Lake Placid

Located in Upstate New York, Lake Placid is a picturesque town that has hosted the 1936 and 1980 Winter Olympic games and serves as a primary Winter Olympic training site.

Lake Placid is a terrific place to sight-see in the couple of days prior to your race. The town is small enough to be engulfed by triathlon fever. Enjoy it while you're there, but there are plenty of ways to escape it on driving tours.

Make a point of driving -- not riding -- the bike course. Along the way, you'll see signs for Olympic ski jump and Bobsled training locations. Do yourself a favor and stop by both locations. Get some friends to join you in an actual dry-land bobsled run. It'll rattle you silly, but it's worth doing once.

Gear Bags and Bike Check-In

When packing for your trip, bring more rather than less.

In my experience, temperatures in the area have varied widely on race day, from a frosty 40 degrees at dawn, to high 80s by early afternoon. Better to have extra clothing choices in your transition bags, just in case the weather is different from what you expected.

Rain and strong winds can arrive on race day, consider that when making your wheel choice. Dealing with strong gusts on steep downhills with slick pavement are more than terrifying on this course.

When checking your bike in on Saturday, cover your handlebars and seat with plastic bags. Even if it doesn't rain overnight, the morning dew will otherwise dampen them. Do not place or tape your nutrition on your bike overnight; wait until morning.

Then take it easy for the rest of the day. You have a big race tomorrow.

Race Morning: Before the Start

The transition area will be bustling with activity before dawn. Try to time your arrival so you can get through the body-marking line and to your bike by about 6:00am. That allows you plenty of time to pump your tires (it's easy to borrow a pump if you don't have one), fill your water bottles and load your nutrition.

Then go check your transition bags to be sure you didn't forget any essentials. Go over your checklist: at a minimum you need a race number, helmet, cycling shoes and running shoes. Missing anything beyond that; too late to worry about it.

Start moving toward the water at 6:30. Enter soon after. The tight entryway gets far too congested with hundreds of racers waiting to the last minute. Go early and find a shallow spot to stand; you won't be treading water endlessly.

Swim

The swim takes place in the calm but tiny Mirror Lake. It's a two lap course, outlined by buoys connected by a white rope that's tantalizingly visible just below the surface.

ighting is easy; you can see land nearby on either side to help orient you. You'll swim nearly to the far end of the lake, so there's no doubt about spotting the turnaround point.

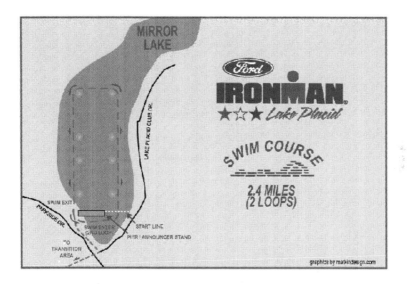

In my opinion, the expansion of the race to more than 2000 participants has overcrowded this swim venue like no other Ironman race. Too little space; too many swimmers. Add to that the popular idea to swim along the little white line for the shortest distance, and you get a nearly unmatched water clobbering scenario. My advice: swim wide, relax, let others fight for position.

Lap one will remain congested no matter where you swim. By the time you start lap two, though, things seem to shake out a bit. More space, less contact, better swimming.

Swim to Bike Transition

Once out of the water, you'll have to go a couple hundred yards to the Olympic Oval transition area. While it seems a long distance, it'll help clear your head a little. When you get your transition bag and enter the transition tent, all seats may be occupied. No problem; just find yourself a spot on grass and change anyway. No real reason to rush, either; you'll have a long day ahead. Just keep moving.

Volunteers will try to help get your bike as you near your rack, and soon enough you'll be exiting the transition area. Be sure to wait until you pass the Special Line before mounting your bike, or you may get a penalty.

Bike

The two-lap bike course is alternatively beautiful, tough, fast, and sometimes all of the above. See map and elevation chart below and on the next page.

After a fast descent outside of the transition area (be careful there), and a speedy, adrenaline-fueled two miles to get out of town the work begins.

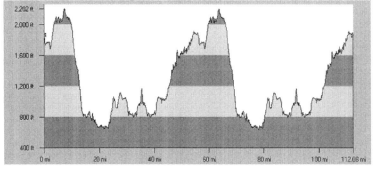

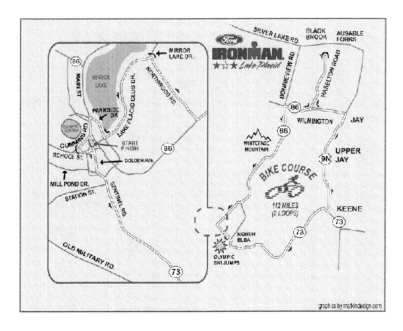

Your first long climb will commence near the Olympic Ski
Jumps, ascending for the next five miles past North Elba.
The climb is forgiving, with several short downhills for
relief, but overall you are climbing.

At the end of your climb you'll encounter a couple of flat
miles past a beautiful stream. Appreciate the view, while
preparing for fun. Next up: a screaming 10k downhill to the
village of Keene. In good weather, go ahead, hammer a
little. You can see speeds of 45mph or more. Just stay to
the right; there will always be hot-rodders passing you at
over 50mph. I'd rather be safe and concede a few seconds.

If the weather is wet and/or windy, be careful, stay under
control. Accidents on this stretch could be very nasty, what
with all the downward momentum.

Sometimes riders experience a shaking of the front wheel, at high speed, and it's hard to control. To avoid this, try to keep your bike stable by hugging the frame with your knees on the way down.

Once you reach Keene, the next eight or so peaceful miles are relatively flat, heading to the town of Jay. Build up some speed here, but don't go crazy. The left turn in Jay will re-introduce you to hills, and you want to withhold some strength.

Your next notable destination is the 14-mile out-and-back on Haselton Road. It's mostly shaded and rolling, sometimes with steep downhills. So steep, that each time I'm coasting down them, I'm also slightly dreading climbing them on the way back. The good news: they aren't as hard to climb as you will think.

After Haselton Road, just a few relatively flat miles on Route 86, then a left turn toward Whiteface Mountain. As 86 approaches the mountain, you'll begin wondering where the terrifying climb you've seen on the course map begins.

Yes, it is there, beginning at about mile 44. But you will be surprised. It doesn't smack you, instead it sneaks up on you, with what ultimately are continuing gentle increases in elevation that are less taxing than you feared. The thing is: they don't provide much relief.

The real climbs occur within miles of the end of lap one. The hills are named, and labeled, Baby Bear. Mama Bear, and Papa Bear. None are too difficult. Get past them, and soon you'll be in town to start again on lap two.

Bike to Run Transition

This one's simple and relatively fast, even if you don't feel like moving too swiftly. Hand your bike to a volunteer, collect your transition bag and find a spot to change into your running shoes. Before you know it, you're off to run a marathon.

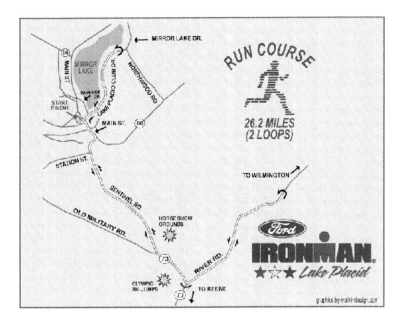

Run

The two-lap 26.2 marathon course has it all. Long straightaways, steep painful declines and inclines, and routing though tree-lined forest roads, see map and elevation chart on the next page.

You'll get a boost from the crowd as you head out of town in the first mile, and then for the next two miles, you're running steady, out of town. By the ski jumps, you'll encounter a quarter-mile swift downhill that your legs may not entirely want to go fast on. Do what you can, then turn left toward the Riverside Road turnaround, about 2.5 miles away.

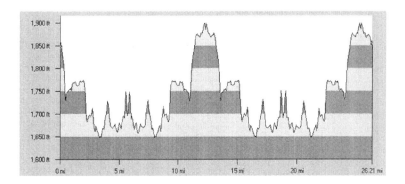

The farther you get on Riverside Road, the less you'll be able to see the course ahead. The turns are constant, so allow yourself to stop worrying where the turnaround point is. Just find that running zone, and enjoy it.

At the turnaround point, you will retrace your steps back to where you started -- including a steep climb at about the 8-mile point that seems unforgiving. When you reach the transition area, you will take a sharp right turn on Lake Placid Club Drive, proceeding to pass the west side of Mirror Lake until you reach the second turnaround about a mile later. Pass it, and return to town to complete your first 13.1 mile lap.

All you have to do next is repeat the loop and you're an Ironman. OK, so it isn't as easy as all that. Just keep moving one step at a time. You will get there.

And you will deserve to be proud. You will be an Ironman.

Details, Schedule, Athletes, Kona Slots

Ironman Race Calendar

Ironman Lake Placid is one of the last races offering
Kona qualifying slots for the current year's race in
Hawaii.

Race	Kona Slots	Race Date
Ironman Malaysia	36	2/27/2010
Ironman New Zealand	75	3/6/2010
Ironman China	50	3/14/2010
Ironman Australia	60	3/28/2010
Ironman South Africa	30	4/25/2010
Ironman St. George	65	5/1/2010
Ironman Lanzarote	60	5/22/2010
Ironman Brazil	50	5/30/2010
Ironman Japan	50	6/13/2010
Ironman France	35	6/27/2010
Ironman Coeur d'Alene	65	6/27/2010
Ironman Germany	120	7/4/2010
Ironman Austria	50	7/4/2010
Ironman Switzerland	72	7/25/2010
Ironman Lake Placid	72	7/25/2010
Ironman Regensburg	50	8/1/2010
Ironman UK	30	8/1/2010
Ironman Louisville	72	8/29/2010
Ironman Canada	72	8/29/2010
Ironman Wisconsin*	72	9/12/2010
Ironman World Championship		10/9/2010
Ironman Florida*	72	11/6/2010
Ironman Arizona*	72	11/21/2010
Ironman Cozumel*	50	11/28/2010
Ironman Western Australia*	40	12/4/2010

* Slots for Kona 2011

Details

- **Race Date**: July 24, 2011
- **Location**: Lake Placid, New York
- **Field size**: around 2700 registered
- **Kona Slots**: 65 for 2011 :
- **2.4 Mile Swim**: 2 laps in Mirror Lake
- **112 Mile Bike:** 2 laps
- **26.2 Marathon:** 2 laps to Riverside Drive
- **Website**: www.ironmanlake placid.com
- **Race Headquarters**: Olympic Skating Loop
- **Notable Area Attractions**: Winter Olympics training facilities, demonstrations and museums
- **Weather**: averages tend to be 60s but conditions have varies from cool rain to extreme heat in different years

Registration: Entry Fee $575

- All participants in the current year's event will have the opportunity to register on-site for the following year's event on the Saturday before the race.
- On-site general registration will open the morning after the event. Individuals may only register themselves; they will not be allowed to register a friend at any event.
- All remaining slots will open for registration online via Active.com at 12:00 p.m. local race site time the day after the current year's race.
- Please check the event website 2 months prior to the race, for more detailed information.

Note: race is typically sold out to general entry immediately; possibilities may exist to enter via the Community Fund; see www.ironmanusa.com

Anticipated Race Week Schedule

Day		Time	Activity
Thursday	7/22/10	7:00 AM	Gatorade Gear Check Mirror Lake
		9:00 AM	Ironman Village
		10:00 AM	Athlete Registration/Packet Pickup
Friday	7/23/10	7:00 AM	Gatorade Gear Check Mirror Lake
		9:00 AM	Ironman Village
		10:00 AM	Athlete Registration/Packet Pickup
		12:30 PM	Pro Athletes Meeting
		2:00 PM	Kids Fun Run
		5:30 PM	Welcome Dinner
		7:30 PM	Mandatory Athlete Meeting
Saturday	7/24/10	7:00 AM	Gatorade Gear Check Mirror Lake
		TBD	Volunteer Team Information Meeting
		9:00 AM	2011 On-Site Registration 2010 Athletes Only
		9:00 AM	Ironman Village
		10:00 AM	Mandatory Bike & Gear Bag Check-in
Sunday	7/25/10	5:00 AM	Transition Zone; Bodymarking
		6:30 AM	Athletes must be at the swim start
		6:50 AM	Pro Race Starts
		7:00 AM	Race Starts
		7:40 AM	First Swimmer out of the water; first bike start
		9:20 AM	Swim Course closes
		12:30 PM	First Bike Returns; First Runner Begins
		3:30 PM	Approx. Time of 1st Finisher
		4:00 PM	Race Day Massage
		5:30 PM	Bike Course Closes
		10:00 PM	Ironman Finish Line Party
		12:00 AM	Race Ends
Monday	7/26/10	8:00 AM	Post-Race Massage
		9:00 AM	2011 for 2010 volunteers and general public
		9:00 AM	2011 Kona Registration, then Rolldown
		9:00 AM	View & Order Race Photos
		12:30 AM	Ironman Awards Banquet

Competitors Completing Each Discipline, By Division

	Start	Finish	DNF	DNF %
M18-24	50	47	3	6%
M25-29	109	107	2	2%
M30-34	256	250	6	2%
M35-39	355	346	9	3%
M40-44	462	440	22	5%
M45-49	370	347	23	6%
M50-54	206	200	6	3%
M55-59	95	89	6	6%
M60-64	34	32	2	6%
M65-69	12	9	3	25%
M70-74	11	10	1	9%
M75-79	1	-	1	100%
MPRO	27	21	6	22%
W18-24	8	7	1	13%
W25-29	64	59	5	8%
W30-34	100	97	3	3%
W35-39	119	115	4	3%
W40-44	141	133	8	6%
W45-49	103	93	10	10%
W50-54	49	43	6	12%
W55-59	15	11	4	27%
W60-64	7	6	1	14%
W65-69	2	-	2	100%
W70+				
WPRO	14	12	2	14%
Total	2,610	2,474	136	5%

Average IMLP Splits and Finish Times by Division

	Swim	Bike	Run	2010
M18-24	1:10:24	6:15:55	4:36:52	12:15:49
M25-29	1:11:58	6:18:08	4:34:39	12:16:50
M30-34	1:13:36	6:15:34	4:32:40	12:14:45
M35-39	1:14:57	6:20:59	4:38:07	12:27:54
M40-44	1:16:36	6:27:56	4:47:56	12:47:26
M45-49	1:17:41	6:29:09	4:48:37	12:51:48
M50-54	1:18:25	6:38:09	4:55:04	13:09:24
M55-59	1:23:05	6:55:00	5:08:30	13:44:31
M60-64	1:22:55	7:04:01	5:32:11	14:18:09
M65-69	1:32:01	7:30:28	5:31:56	14:56:05
M70-74	1:31:19	7:11:58	5:44:34	14:45:28
M75-79				
MPRO	1:00:44	5:07:41	3:15:49	9:30:15
W18-24	1:12:18	7:05:40	4:55:00	13:30:40
W25-29	1:18:12	6:55:10	4:52:25	13:16:50
W30-34	1:15:37	6:55:22	4:49:04	13:14:57
W35-39	1:19:11	7:01:21	4:54:02	13:31:58
W40-44	1:18:54	6:53:45	5:01:01	13:29:57
W45-49	1:20:06	7:04:01	4:59:41	13:42:33
W50-54	1:23:30	7:16:33	5:16:19	14:16:47
W55-59	1:26:47	7:29:17	5:45:00	15:00:50
W60-64	1:20:50	7:12:34	4:55:48	13:54:08
W65-69				
W70+				
WPRO	1:03:29	5:36:22	3:30:30	10:16:51
Grand Total	1:16:49	6:34:20	4:47:49	12:54:16

Ironman Race Comparison: Average Finish Times

	Swim	Bike	Run	Total
St. George	1:21	7:02	5:07	13:47
Wisconsin	1:20	6:29	5:10	13:16
Malaysia	1:26	6:21	5:19	13:15
Cozumel	1:08	6:39	5:11	13:11
UK	1:24	6:53	4:34	13:10
Coeur d'Alene	1:20	6:27	5:05	13:08
Canada	1:17	6:23	5:08	13:00
Lanzarote	1:09	6:59	4:38	13:00
Lake Placid	**1:16**	**6:34**	**4:47**	**12:54**
South Africa	1:18	6:18	5:00	12:52
Louisville	1:23	6:21	4:48	12:51
Arizona	1:20	6:08	4:58	12:43
Florida	1:21	6:02	4:57	12:37
France	1:17	6:24	4:34	12:32
New Zealand	1:09	6:17	4:36	12:15
Australia	1:04	6:15	4:54	12:13
Brazil	1:20	6:03	4:40	11:59
W Australia	1:11	5:52	4:48	11:52
Austria	1:15	5:46	4:31	11:45
Germany	1:11	5:42	4:34	11:39
Kona	1:13	5:56	4:17	11:37
Switzerland	1:15	5:48	4:17	11:30

Kona Slot Allocation

Your age on race day will put you in one of several 5-year span age divisions, e.g., at age 48, you would compete in the 45-49 Division.

The number of available slots per race are allocated among the Age Divisions and Pro athletes using the following guidelines as described at ironmanusa.com:

"At least one Kona slot shall be allocated IN FULL-DISTANCE EVENTS to each five-year age-group category in which any age group athlete sends in an application, both male and female, per the age group categories listed.

Be aware that some age groups may be combined for the allocation of a Kona slot at the sole discretion of the race director. If there are no athletes entered in the race in a particular age group, then that slot will be moved to the largest populated age group in that same gender. For additional age group slots, slot allocation shall be representative of the actual number of age group applicants in each category in the race.

As an example, if 8% of the age-group applicants are females 40-44, then 8% of these slots would be allocated in the female 40-44 category. Please note that at 10 percent of Ford Ironman World Championship slots at full-distance events are allocated to Professionals, i.e., qualifying spots, eight are reserved for pros.

Note: All athletes must be present at Hawaii Registration to claim their spot."

Ironman Lake Placid Kona Slot Allocation 2009-2010

IMLP	2009	2010
M18-24	1	2
M25-29	3	3
M30-34	5	6
M35-39	8	8
M40-44	9	10
M45-49	8	8
M50-54	5	5
M55-59	3	3
M60-64	1	1
M65-69	1	1
M70-74	1	1
M75-79		
MPRO	4	1
W18-24	1	1
W25-29	2	2
W30-34	4	3
W35-39	3	3
W40-44	4	4
W45-49	3	3
W50-54	2	1
W55-59	1	1
W60-64		1
W65-69		
W75+		
WPRO	3	3
Total	72	71

With more than 2600 triathletes compete in Ironman Lake Placid, the odds of getting a Kona slot get lower each year. Things get tougher: in the highly popular Divisions, between ages 30-34, 35-39, 40-44, 45-49, and 50-54, for example, you'll need to finish among the top 3% or so of the group.

For the real Reality Check: look at the times turned in by the athletes that qualified for Kona in the 2010 Ironman Lake Placid.

Note: the above comments to the contrary, do not get discouraged when you see some extraordinary times posted by athletes in your age Division.

Don't let yourself be intimidated if you feel the gap between your current performance and ability and target qualifying times is too great.

You want to improve, you want to know the goals you're shooting for. If the goal is Kona – and it is if you're reading this – this is the starting point.

Most importantly, remember: every qualifying athlete listed on the following pages at one point could only dream of winning a Kona slot. Through hard and efficient training, they achieved the goal. With determination and perseverance, you will, too.

Last Kona Qualifying Time by Year, by Division

IMLP	2009	2010
M18-24	9:49:51	10:31:47
M25-29	10:00:35	9:48:44
M30-34	9:58:58	9:59:07
M35-39	10:08:44	9:52:20
M40-44	10:12:11	10:02:07
M45-49	10:36:57	10:23:08
M50-54	11:09:33	10:46:41
M55-59	11:19:37	11:31:08
M60-64	13:55:54	11:42:26
M65-69	16:02:40	13:22:39
M70-74	14:18:45	14:18:13
M75-79		
MPRO	9:15:27	8:39:34
W18-24	12:33:37	11:12:05
W25-29	11:34:23	10:44:41
W30-34	11:06:04	10:46:58
W35-39	11:11:06	10:55:46
W40-44	11:16:50	11:15:21
W45-49	11:41:26	11:00:03
W50-54	11:49:06	11:53:29
W55-59	13:58:02	12:05:21
W60-64		13:00:34
W65-69		
W75+		
WPRO	10:05:59	9:53:39

All Lake Placid Kona Qualifying Times by Division

Division	Swim	Bike	Run	Finish
M18-24	1:02:34	5:06:41	3:04:37	9:20:27
M18-24	1:18:18	5:32:30	3:32:05	10:31:47
M25-29	57:26:00	5:11:20	3:17:10	9:33:13
M25-29	57:33:00	5:08:58	3:25:29	9:36:56
M25-29	57:22:00	5:26:04	3:17:42	9:48:44
M30-34	55:23:00	5:04:41	3:11:19	9:18:22
M30-34	57:21:00	5:20:39	3:18:31	9:42:22
M30-34	1:00:28	5:18:07	3:15:28	9:42:42
M30-34	58:40:00	5:18:55	3:18:59	9:43:43
M30-34	1:04:29	5:23:54	3:18:31	9:56:05
M30-34	1:05:11	5:22:09	3:18:22	9:59:07
M35-39	57:53:00	5:20:15	3:01:34	9:27:30
M35-39	1:01:05	5:13:10	3:13:30	9:34:33
M35-39	59:08:00	5:23:41	3:07:08	9:37:00
M35-39	1:00:04	5:15:18	3:18:27	9:40:07
M35-39	57:15:00	5:30:53	3:08:03	9:43:56
M35-39	1:02:07	5:14:21	3:25:02	9:47:27
M35-39	51:58:00	5:29:03	3:24:15	9:52:13
M35-39	1:10:35	5:23:05	3:11:25	9:52:20
M40-44	55:21:00	5:14:12	3:18:24	9:34:42
M40-44	58:52:00	5:21:10	3:09:05	9:37:19
M40-44	52:54:00	5:24:27	3:19:33	9:43:42
M40-44	50:54:00	5:36:12	3:14:07	9:48:12
M40-44	57:16:00	5:20:29	3:24:13	9:49:31
M40-44	1:08:53	5:30:07	3:13:32	9:59:36
M40-44	1:06:24	5:26:15	3:19:35	9:59:44
M40-44	1:01:22	5:24:48	3:27:05	10:00:08
M40-44	55:12:00	5:25:20	3:35:05	10:01:40
M40-44	1:10:48	5:32:22	3:12:01	10:02:07
M45-49	59:24:00	5:20:06	3:24:12	9:51:32
M45-49	1:02:26	5:17:17	3:38:38	10:08:22
M45-49	1:08:44	5:15:54	3:37:21	10:12:50
M45-49	52:17:00	5:37:39	3:39:13	10:19:12
M45-49	1:08:44	5:25:13	3:37:47	10:20:18
M45-49	1:08:10	5:34:11	3:29:24	10:21:02
M45-49	57:13:00	5:34:07	3:43:19	10:21:06
M45-49	1:02:48	5:31:40	3:39:38	10:23:08

All Lake Placid Kona Qualifying Times by Division

Division	Swim	Bike	Run	Finish
M50-54	1:07:31	5:28:19	3:43:27	10:29:39
M50-54	1:03:16	5:35:11	3:46:37	10:33:17
M50-54	1:03:47	5:32:21	3:55:59	10:39:58
M50-54	1:07:41	5:50:46	3:26:53	10:42:14
M50-54	1:03:07	5:51:29	3:39:59	10:46:41
M55-59	1:14:33	5:26:07	3:52:37	10:43:52
M55-59	1:11:29	5:39:56	4:00:32	11:03:22
M55-59	1:03:37	6:10:53	4:01:37	11:31:08
M60-64	1:11:04	5:50:19	4:28:54	11:42:26
M65-69	1:59:16	7:03:38	4:04:43	13:22:39
M70-74	1:26:38	7:22:58	5:10:54	14:18:13
MPRO	55:06:00	4:38:03	3:01:24	8:39:34
W18-24	1:06:31	6:25:55	3:30:04	11:12:05
W25-29	55:21:00	5:39:45	3:29:36	10:11:32
W25-29	1:00:29	5:57:37	3:36:08	10:44:41
W30-34	1:06:23	5:58:18	3:31:26	10:43:23
W30-34	1:03:56	5:58:33	3:35:35	10:45:35
W30-34	57:46:00	5:57:47	3:41:02	10:46:58
W35-39	1:09:15	5:58:38	3:18:37	10:34:33
W35-39	1:08:56	5:59:26	3:27:33	10:45:20
W35-39	1:08:53	5:50:39	3:48:08	10:55:46
W40-44	57:15:00	5:56:08	3:52:49	10:56:50
W40-44	1:05:13	5:56:39	3:53:15	11:02:22
W40-44	1:10:30	5:58:05	3:57:55	11:14:20
W40-44	1:17:04	5:51:12	3:57:09	11:15:21
W45-49	1:02:45	5:50:59	3:41:07	10:43:54
W45-49	1:00:49	6:03:05	3:46:23	10:58:20
W45-49	1:09:00	5:53:25	3:49:49	11:00:03
W50-54	1:16:48	5:54:26	4:30:54	11:53:29
W55-59	1:20:20	6:41:01	3:51:15	12:05:21
W60-64	1:18:54	6:18:16	5:07:29	13:00:34
WPRO	57:22:00	5:37:30	3:03:37	9:44:18
WPRO	57:35:00	5:25:45	3:22:46	9:51:31
WPRO	57:27:00	5:27:02	3:23:12	9:53:39

Kona Slot #1: Ironman USA Lake Placid 2002

My Ironman experience, from the first one in 1997, until late last year, can be summarized by words from Lance Armstrong's book, It's Not About the Bike:

"People ask me why I ride my bike for six hours a day; what is the pleasure? The answer is that I don't do it for the pleasure. I do it for the pain. In my most painful moments on the bike, I am at my most self-aware and self-defining. There is a point in every race when a rider encounters the real opponent and realizes that it's...himself. You might say pain is my chosen way of exploring the human heart."

My Ironman races were never about qualifying for Hawaii. That was Big League, usually an hour or more faster than my finish times. Kona was out of reach, but I was more than happy to race Ironman for those moments of self-awareness and exploration.

But things began to change last Fall, when I began breaking personal barriers. Three sub-3 hour marathons (including a 2:54 at Boston 2002), and a 19th place AG finish at Ironman New Zealand 2002 (20 minutes from a Kona slot) indicated I was in new territory as an athlete, and maybe, just maybe, ready to try to earn entry to The Ironman World Championships at Kona.

I approached this Ironman much differently than previous races. I dramatically shifted training time from the run to the bike, and stepped up the hours from an average of seven per week to nearly ten hours. I felt more ready than ever by mid-July.

I had raced Ironman USA in 1999, and finished in 12:22. I arrived in Lake Placid aiming to finish below the 10:42 time that earned the last Kona slot in my M40-44 age group in 2001.

Swim

I always have a single goal in the swim – exit the water fresh, so I could take advantage of my better events – and this race would be no different. Temperatures were in the high 50s as the cannon fired at 7am, starting the race for 1754 contestants.

Despite the congestion in tiny Mirror Lake , the contact at the start was minimal, and I stayed away from aggressive action by swimming wide. I just tried to swim straight. Timing data supplied by Marc Roy of Sportstats, shows that I was 794th to complete lap 1 of the swim, typical of recent efforts.

On lap 2, I think I followed the same person the entire way, buoy to buoy, and interestingly, exited the water in 793rd place in 1:10. You don't get more consistent than that.

The run to Transition 1 is about ¼ mile, I ran fast to shave time, and it worked. At 0:05:31, my T1 was 306th fastest, and if the data is correct, I passed 97 people in the transition area on the way to the bike start.

Bike

My shift to bike emphasis was obvious in this year's training log – I averaged 30 miles per week in 2001, but was up to 85 miles per week in 2002, with several 150+ mile weeks. These totals are low compared to most fast riders, but they gave me the confidence that I would significantly improve on the 6:35 bike time I posted at Ironman USA in 1999.

The Ironman USA bike course is technical, with continuous rolling and turning terrain, and an elevation change of 7624 feet over two 56 mile laps. My bike strategy was probably too simple: ride in control, maintain high cadence where possible, and don't implode on the last ten climbing miles.

Once on the bike, I rode based on feel, and I felt aggressive. I just wanted to attack. Out of the saddle on the crests of hills, I drove past other riders. They may have thought I was crazy, but most weren't able to catch me to let me know.

I finished lap 1 feeling strong, with a time of 2:41:29, or about 20.8 mph. Data for the first 56 miles was uploaded to the Internet on www.ironmanlive.com. Friends, including Joe Foster, multiple-time Kona qualifier and my race advisor, were watching. With the live data, they knew far more than I did about what was happening, including that I had the 204th fastest bike split for the lap.

After seeing the lap 1 results, Joe sent an email to several Iron friends, saying:

"Based on a very quick scan of the top 60 (M40-44) at the 'half bike' posting, only 25 seem to have a pace that is interesting. Key for Ray (at about 57th M40-44 and moving up) will be holding his pace against the tide of deterioration that will sweep the field after the 'lap of exuberance' is done and reality sets in (Lap 1.5-2). He must be feeding off the energy of all those racers he is passing as he moves up the field!"

Things got interesting just after lap 2 began, as it started to rain. Wet road and this course don't mix well, and that meant all riders had to slow down. That didn't prevent bloody crashes, which led me to ride even more cautiously as the rain began pounding harder and harder. But I had energy to spare, and had no problem powering through the hard climbs between mile 101 and 111.

Part of my energy reserve came from having the right gearing. I had obsessed before the race about which cassette to use – a 12-23 for speed, or 12-25 to better manage the climbs. Never the shy one, my brother-in-law called his friend George Hincapie (Lance Armstrong's lieutenant on Team US Postal), at the Tour de France, to pose the question. The reply from Hincapie, shortly after his epic pull during Stage 11 in the Pyrenees: "Go with the 12x25. I have never heard of anyone regretting having one more gear."

He was right. There is nothing like the feeling of having climbed 7600 feet on the bike over 111 miles, and feeling more ready than ever to run a marathon.

With the rain, my pace did deteriorate on lap 2, but the same was true for just about everyone. I finished with the 276th fastest lap 2, for 246th best bike time overall at 5:41:37. This was my best bike positioning ever, and I had passed 288 racers along the way.

Run

After a 49th fastest T2 overall in 0:02:13, I sprinted (not an exaggeration) onto the run course in 308th place.

With the lap 2 bike data in hand from www.ironmanlive.com, Joe emailed the group again as I started running:

"Ray is off the bike in 47th M40-44 position! VERY promising is the fact that he is near dead-on his time goals and his T-2 was *very* fast. From 'cyber-land,' this indicates that he is executing on his race plan and taking free time from his lesser competitors.

"My forecast: Ray gets 13/14 positions on the basis of attrition (fast swimmers on the decline, poor second bike laps and assumptions based on long T-2s). He will need to throw everything into the run to battle it out with the remaining 33 racers."

That's exactly what I did. The 2:54 at Boston in April finally convinced me that I'm a Real Runner. I tore into the run telling myself that there were few who could run better, and I planned to prove it.

The two-lap run course is among the more challenging on the Ironman circuit, with steep climbs on two sections, and other twists and turns. The cool rain ended as my run began, and the sun came out, for a dramatic heat increase, impacting body temperature regulation for all competitors.

The first 13 miles were a blur of spotting the next guy, checking to see if he was in my age group, passing him, repeat. At the turnarounds, I checked to see how many in my age group were ahead, and the numbers weren't significant. I kept picking M40-44s off one at a time, and rarely was anyone able to hold my pace for long.

My worst period was between miles 14 and 20, when it seems my systems were out of balance. Art Hutchinson, Ironman veteran, was watching on the sidelines, and noted I was both flush in the face, and had goose bumps on my arms. My vision was going blurry, and for a few minutes I thought I was in trouble. I began devouring cola, Gatorade and oranges at aid stations, and felt somewhat better. The good news was, I was still passing people, but my pace had slowed.

I only checked my watch at the mile 21 point, and saw 9:50 had elapsed. With 5.2 miles to go, I would have to dig in to finish comfortably within last year's qualifying time of 10:42. I picked up the pace, and drove myself back into town, continuing the drop the occasional M40-44 athlete who had surrendered to the heat. Former Ironman Canada winner Michael McCormack once told me his Ironman mantra: as the race goes longer, I get stronger. At this point, I knew what he meant.

I saw Art at mile 24, he shouted 'it's yours if you want it! Run!' I turned up the speed and motored toward the finish. On the last mile, I spotted a group of several runners well in front of me. Too far ahead, I thought. To my surprise, I caught all but one.

With great happiness, exhaustion and relief, I ran into the finish area on the 400-meter speed skating Olympic Oval, having passed 198 runners on the marathon course, including 34 in my age group. My 3:33 marathon was 55th fastest of the day, and a PR by 6 minutes. At 10:33:51, I finished 13th M40-44, and ultimately, about 15 minutes ahead of the last qualifying finisher.

The next day, I collected my Kona slot.

As each day goes by, I'm increasingly overwhelmed by what this achievement means. I never dreamed that running a 4:41 Chicago Marathon in October 1994 would begin an endurance racing career that would lead me on an eventual path to Kona.
It's been an amazing journey.

Vineman Ironman 1997 11:34:06
Ironman Canada 1997 11:47:40
Ironman Europe 1998 11:40:31
Ironman Switzerland 1998 12:46:07
Ironman Canada 1998 12:42:27
Ironman New Zealand 1999 12:08:04
Ironman USA 1999 12:22:38
Ironman Canada 1999 11:59:36
Ironman Florida 1999 11:15:57
Ironman California 2000 13:35:23
Ironman Florida 2000 11:09:40
Ironman Austria 2001 11:26:55
Ironman Florida 2001 10:40:13
Ironman New Zealand 2002 10:41:58
Ironman USA 2002 10:33:51

What's made the difference in performance? In short: increased biking/less running, more high intensity workouts, increased training time overall, stronger/leaner physique, and strong mental determination.

Ironman USA Lake Placid, New York, July 2003

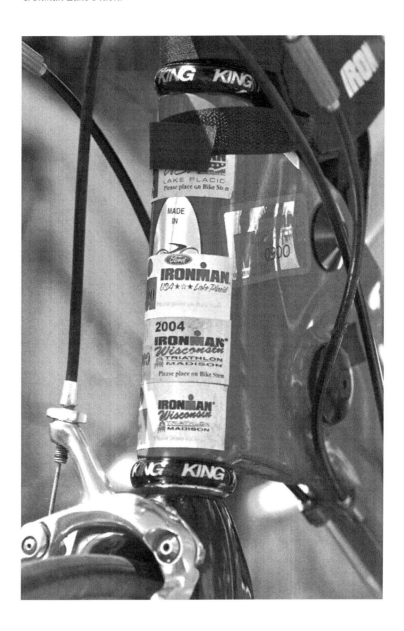

On the evening before the 2003 Ironman USA in Lake Placid, athletes tuned into the Weather Channel, hoping the gloomy race day forecast would change. Doppler radar showed thick rain clouds and forecasts predicted winds from the west of up to 30mph. I'm certain we all had the same thought: heavy wind and rain like that isn't sustainable, is it?

At 6am on race morning, it was clear the wind wasn't going to back down, and I made a last minute decision to remove my disc wheel set from my yellow Softride Powerwing, and replace them with four-spoke wheels. The wind whipped up more as I walked to the swim start area, and I patted myself on the back for making a good equipment decision, not knowing that I had also made a mistake that might impact my race.

After finishing preparations in the transition area, I joined 1835 starters and waded into Mirror Lake. As I had done at this race in 1999 and 2002, I placed myself in about the middle of the pack for the swim start, and waited for the mayhem of the two-loop swim to begin.

Months earlier, I had expected to enter the swim portion of IMUSA in peak form, in search of a swim personal best. Swimming is by far my weakest leg, and I've been determined to improve it. But a string of injuries starting last December had served to keep me out of the water for weeks at a time. The latest injury impacted my right ribs/shoulder, reducing it to a weak pull, at best, after missing most of the six weeks prior to the race.

Swim

What I lacked in swim fitness I hoped to make up for with better positioning in the pack, and with the benefits of a new wetsuit. So from the start, I went right into the middle of the fray and tried to hold my own. The good news: I felt great in the water, flowing smoothly, and stroking freely. Unfortunately, my right shoulder was not yet ready to handle the full stress of a 2.4 mile swim, so it was less effective, reduced at times to just stabilizing me in the water. Still, I hit the beach after the first lap seeing 35 minutes on the clock, and was happy with that as I dove back in to start lap 2.

The second lap felt great. I'm used to tiring in the last half mile of the swim, but I was surprisingly pleased to feel like I was getting stronger with every stroke on the way back to the beach. I passed about 100 swimmers on lap two, and knew I'd have plenty of energy for the rest of the race.

Still in the water, I began to think ahead to the bike ride, and was again congratulating myself for switching wheels, when I realized the problem: the disc wheel I had removed had a 12-25 cassette, and the four-spoke wheel cassette had a 12-23 – perfect for training in the flat Chicago area, but not ideal on the hilly Lake Placid bike course. Uh oh. With no option, I decided I would have to make the best of it – I had always wondered what it would be like to race an Ironman in 12-23, and now I would get my chance. I only hoped it wouldn't destroy my quads for the run.

Coming out of the water, I was happy to see 1:12:19 on the clock, much better than a 1:19:15 with comparable swim fitness at Ironman USA 1999.

Next, I ran the few hundred meters to the Olympic speed skating oval transition area. It was raining lightly, and the trees were whipping back and forth in the wind as I tried to get through transition quickly. Heading to the start of the bike course, I heard an announcement about a downpour in

Keene, urging extreme caution. Extreme caution was right. Within 30 minutes, things got dangerous on the course.

Bike

I break IMUSA's two 56-mile loop bike course into several sections: climbs out of town to the 8 mile point, followed by a winding, screaming downhill of about 10k to the town of Keene; about nine flat miles to the town of Jay; five miles net uphill to the a 14 mile rolling out-and-back on Haselton Road; then about twelve miles climbing back to town past Whiteface Mountain on route 86.

After climbing for several miles out of town, I rolled into the steep downhill to Keene, where I had enjoyed speeds of 50mph on dry roads in 2002. This time, however, the crosswind was gusting up to 30 mph, rain was falling and the roads were slick. In no time, I realized I was going too fast, and tried to get the bike under control, but to no avail. With the wind smacking me repeatedly like the back of a celestial hand, my front wheel started wobbling, and I was being literally pushed me sideways back and forth on the road. Tapping the brakes increased the instability, and I was hurtling faster and faster downhill toward certain disaster.

Images of Joseba Beloki crashing in Stage 9 of this year's Tour de France kept flashing before my eyes, and I was certain that it was not a matter of if, but when I would crash. I was only trying to delay the inevitable as long as possible.

To make things worse, the road ahead veered to the left, and with a wobbly front wheel, there seemed to be no way I could make that turn. I was terrified as never before (and many other racers later confessed the same fears).

Miraculously, I made the turn upright, got the bike back under control, and rode the rest of the way downhill with hands on the brakes.

Extremely relieved to arrive in one piece at the base of the descent in Keene, I followed the course east with a delightfully strong tailwind, which brought me to the 24 mile turn in Jay with about 62 minutes elapsed on the bike. Fast! That was the last time I had fun on the bike course, however.

The wind just wasn't going to quit, and it was clearly impacting everybody. Entering the Haselton Road out and back, I began to see the leaders returning from the turnaround, and they were more spread out than usual. When I reached the turnaround and headed west, I understood why: the headwinds were wicked, and were pushing riders every which way. I also understood that there was no way to avoid them for the remaining trip back to town through intermittent rain.

The climb past Whiteface mountain takes riders past beautiful mountains, streams and waterfalls, views which helped to minimize any frustration caused by conditions. Still, the wind whipping off the mountains had the potential to stop riders dead in their tracks, or to push them abruptly to the side without warning. There was no sitting back to idly spin the climbs; you had to be on alert every second or the wind could knock you over.

Interesting note: in 2002 the word 'Pain' and a forward arrow were painted on the crest of a hill about 4 miles from Lake Placid, indicating that the upcoming climbs would hurt. This year, I noticed someone had altered the word to read 'Rain', and it was true — rain was ahead, and it wasn't stopping. But I got through the final climbs with ease, and passing through the 'Hot Corner' – the best place for spectators to see riders in downtown Lake Placid – I ended lap 1 in 2:47:38. Prior to the race, I had planned for a time about 6 minutes faster, but was not disappointed, given the weather out there.

Back on the steep downhill to Keene, I wasn't going to make the same mistake twice. This time, I slowly and defensively rode the brakes to town, and watched rider after rider fly by me on the left. I was happy to lose time to them in order to arrive at the bottom safely.

After the Haselton Road out and back, I turned into the wind at mile 100 for twelve final uphill miles into the relentless headwind. These are among the most challenging final miles on any Ironman bike course, and you really need an extra gear for it. I didn't have that extra gear because of my wheel change, so I had no choice but to push ahead. Surprisingly, I felt great, staying in the seat and spinning to pass rider after rider. But would the extra effort come back to haunt me on the run?

Soon, I was back in town, steering into transition to finish a 5:50:34 bike ride. My lap 2 was 3:02:57, only two minutes slower than lap 2 in the 2002 race, which featured heavy downpours, but no wind. Even though my overall ride was nine minutes slower in 2003, I felt like I had actually ridden better and stronger than in 2002. Race statistics confirmed it: I had the 200th fastest overall bike, compared to 244th in 2002, and I had passed more than 600 people on the bike course.

Feeling strong and ready to run, I tore through the second transition in 2:12, 77th fastest, and entered the run course in 274th place. Delighted to spot my 13 year-old daughter Amanda at the side of the road with friends, I detoured for a quick hug, then went back to business.

Run

The run course is two 13.1 mile loops consisting of 2 miles out of town to a downhill by the Olympic ski jumping hills, an out and back through the woods to a turnaround at about mile 6.5 on River Road, uphill back towards town at mile 9, a short steep climb at mile 11, and an out and back on Mirror Lake road before heading back to lap two.

Starting the run, I felt as fresh as I had in 2002, when I ran an Ironman Personal Best 3:33:46. My mission on the run was to stay steady, and keep passing people. Reaching the 6.5 mile turnaround in just over 42 minutes meant I was running 7:47/minute miles; excellent! Then nature conspired to try to slow everyone down: rain became heavier, then it became a monsoon. I kept going as the pounding rain continued, then noticed the road had become a stream with water approaching ankle deep in some places.

It was interesting how the Ironmen and Ironwomen around me reacted to the torrential rain: there was practically no grumbling whatsoever. On a day where competitors had been plagued with incredibly frustrating wind and rain, while few people were happy about it, people just kept racing. We all dealt with it. It made us stronger. There was no drama. It was simple: we were going to finish.

In what seemed like no time, I was at the mile 13 checkpoint in town, still feeling strong after a 1:44:00 half marathon. My pace slowed in lap two, but still, the next 47 minutes flew by, and soon I was heading home from the turnaround, feeling strong. I could finally toss the big worry aside: it was clear that being forced to use the 12-23 gearing was not hurting my run.

Passing Amanda for a final time at mile 24, I smiled, and she smiled, knowing the next time I'd see her was at the finish. I had been picking up speed relative to the field, and as I entered the Olympic speed skating oval, I had passed 138 people on the marathon to cross the line 136th overall in 10:49:06.

Throughout the remainder of the night, another 1500 or so athletes braved the rain and wind to cross the line themselves. We had all been through a day unlike any we could have imagined, and yet we had persevered and finished. We all had reason to be proud. And many of us will be back in 2004 . . .

Kona Slot #4: Ironman USA Lake Placid 2004

Two weeks before the 2004 Ironman USA in Lake Placid, NY, I was on the other side of the country, watching the US Olympic Track and Field Trials in Sacramento California. On an evening where world class athletes were making the impossible look easy in a variety of running events, what stood out most was the high jump competition. The bar kept rising well beyond the height of the jumpers, ridiculously high. Yet the jumpers routinely defied the law of gravity, launching themselves to new levels.

It got me thinking about how high I've been able to raise the bar in my own racing since 1994. On reflection, I realized that in the last 10 years there were at least three different stages in my racing career where I was convinced I probably could raise the bar no further, and as of summer 2004, I was again stuck.

Marathon Plateau Ranges:
* 1995 to 1999 — 3:10 to 3:14
* 2000 to 2001 — 3:04 to 3:06
* 2002 to present 2:54 to 2:59

Ironman Plateau Ranges:
* 1997 to 2000 – 11 to 12 hours (and in May 2000, 13 hours. Ouch)
* 2000 to 2001 — Low 11-hours
* 2001 to July 2004– 10:33 to 10:50

At each plateau, I really had the feeling that maybe it couldn't get any better. Or maybe that it would require too much of a commitment, or radical change, to improve. And after the 2002 season, though I didn't want to admit it, that feeling kept creeping back. In each of the last two years, I've been asking myself: am I as good as I will ever be? is it possible to get better? If so, how? These questions are usually followed by: I'm getting older, with less available time; is it possible I might be on my way to getting worse?

For perspective, my personal best Ironman was achieved in Lake Placid in 2002: 10:33, with a 1:10 swim, 5:40 bike on the hilly course, 3:33 marathon (my best ever in an Ironman). I was at the top of my game that year, what I considered my best shape ever, I had finished 13th in the M40-44 age group on a tough course. While I've done well enough to qualify for Kona two times since then with several sub-11 hour finishes, I hadn't come within 5 minutes of that PR. Also, after a horrible start to the 2004 season, I was really concerned that my best racing was behind me.

Recent weeks have delivered definitive answers to those questions and concerns. Specifically, I lowered my Ironman PR by 21 minutes to 10:12:22 at Ironman USA Lake Placid with bike and marathon PRs in July, and set 1500 meter swim and 10k run PRs on my way to my first 'podium' at a local Olympic Distance triathlon two weeks later.

The main question people have been asking after raising the bar in recent weeks: what did you do differently?

1. Training Time (more? are you kidding?)

The thing I did not do was spend more time training. Not that it's a choice. As I get older, my kids get older, the job gets more demanding, there's less time in the day.

As you saw in my 2002 training log, one of the things I concluded was the basis of that strong racing year was an increase in training time and miles. I had increased my average training time in the first 30 weeks of 2002 prior to Ironman USA to about 9.5 hours per week. By contrast, over the same period in 2004, I averaged less than 8 hours per week. Yes, both years had begun with low volume weeks, and had exceeded the weekly averages before race day, but still, there was a clear difference.

Avg Hours/Week preceding Ironman USA Lake Placid (Bike, Run, Swim, Total)

- 2002: 4:14:28, 3:26:01, 1:52:08, 9:32:37
- 2003: 3:21:15, 3:21:31, 0:46:22, 7:29:08
- 2004: 3:00:08, 3:52:53, 0:58:02, 7:51:03

So you couldn't say more training time was behind the improvements. But was it better training time?

2. Higher Quality Training

I don't even need to say it. With fewer hours, you need to get more out of them through higher quality training. But it's easier said than done. What does higher quality mean? For me this year, it meant raising the bar higher, and demanding to achieve higher speeds, regardless of time limits, particularly on the bike.

Just as I had racing plateaus, I also have had training plateaus. I remember in the late 1990s when averaging 20 mph on a single bike training ride was a huge deal. I remember later telling myself that 20mph must be the minimum, and it took a long time to get there. This year, I wanted to be comfortable averaging 21mph on training rides from 20 to 100 miles. That's a 5% improvement, and remembering what an effort it was to even get to that 20mph level, it seemed a real stretch.

But that goal became the focus, and to get there I had to try to find any advantage possible, with better form, higher cadence, or more strength pushing bigger gears. I forced myself to not be intimidated by seeing 25 mph on the bike computer, for example. You know how you can tell yourself: that's too fast! Try this: get to an impossible speed, then block out those negative thoughts; tell yourself YOU CAN. Then try to spend more time at that speed. What seemed beyond reach can soon seem normal, and you don't need a million training hours to get there.

3. Attitude

Even limitless training time and an abundance of hammer training sessions do not guarantee you good performance on race day. I know people who claim to train 20 to 25 hours per week who fizzle the second they pin their bib number on. I have trained with people who can endlessly crush me in workouts but cannot seem to get it together to have a good race. Putting in the time and effort may be enough to finish, but it's not enough to guarantee you the result you want or deserve.

The missing ingredient is Attitude. You need to head onto the race course knowing what you want to do, with the determination to do it, and the will to succeed even when the bar is seemingly beyond reach. I think back to those high jumpers at the Olympic Trials, each facing a bar that is physically higher than they are. Anyone would say it's impossible to get over something taller than yourself; these athletes say: let me at it! And they fly over it.

utting it All Together

I did not have that will to succeed as the season opened. In a half marathon that I eventually finished with a time that I wouldn't even consider good for a training run, I had absolutely the wrong attitude. I ran defensively, hoping it wouldn't fall apart, and of course it did. My attitude, not my conditioning, had let it happen.

By July, I had the opposite approach. I went to Lake Placid buoyed by the new speeds I was seeing in my bike training, and with a May marathon finish under my belt that I knew few on the course could touch. The night before the race, I just had this feeling: I could not wait to get on the bike and run course and see how fast I could go. On the bike course, I was flying faster than ever before (eventually a 15 minute Lake Placid PR), and not concerned that I was pushing too hard. Determined to PR on the run, even at mile 8 I was saying to myself not the usual 'I hope I can hold on,' but 'I've never felt better at this point.' Confidence from training and the right attitude on the course can make the difference.

I was racing blind in Lake Placid – my watch had been kicked off during the swim, and my bike computer didn't work. I just went on feel. It was only when I saw the clock at about mile 24 did I know that I would PR by possibly 20 minutes or more. That was a significant movement of the bar. If you had asked me to consider it before the race, I would have said that was well over my head.

The top three US women high jump finishers that night in Sacramento all successfully sailed over 6 feet, 4.75 inches (1.95 meters). Impossible. But nobody told them, and now they will compete in Athens. Their lesson: don't limit yourself, and you can achieve your own impossible thing.

Looking back on my racing over the last 10 years, I see that too many times I stalled, thinking I might never get better. And, honestly, I will probably think the same thing again someday. But I need to keep in mind, and you should too: history can repeat, the bar can be raised, get your training and attitude right, and you can sail over that bar again and again.

Ironman USA Lake Placid, New York, July 2005

Ironman USA 2005 was going to be my 25th Ironman finish, nearly coinciding with my triathlon debut 10 years earlier, and my 5th race in Lake Placid. A lot had been accomplished over those races and those years. Some great races, some really bad ones. From the desert of Arizona to the mountains of Zurich. From the lowest lows to the highest highs. From a nervous Ironman distance debut in 1997 to Kona.

But after so many races, is there anything new left to experience? The answer is yes. There's so much more that surrounds the race itself, so much that can truly enhance the racing experience. That's what I wanted from this 25th Ironman – a new experience, a new beginning, a way to keep it fresh and fun going forward.

The amazing thing is, when you open your eyes beyond the race, the goals, the splits, the transitions and the slots, there is so much to see.

At a typical North American Ironman, there are about 2000 athletes preparing to race, each with their own reasons for being there. Some want to finish something they once thought impossible. Some want to race to raise awareness for a worthy cause. Some want to go faster than they did the last time. Some want to qualify for Kona. Some want to win.

Some want to finish just because it's fun. That was me, this time, this year, at my 25th Ironman.

Not that I wouldn't have minded racing with greater aspirations, but this season has been one of compromise, less time for triathlon, more time for other important things, and that's the way it is. I entered the race averaging about 6 hours training per week, typically with 2-3 days off each week as Lake Placid approached. You do the best with what you have.

Race Morning – A Beautiful, Foggy Dawn

I started the day differently than usual. Rather than the mind-numbing early wake-up call, the frantic obsessing over last-minute things, and rushing to transition, I slept in an extra hour. I calmly walked the half mile to transition, looking at the moon in the sky and the fog coming off of calm Mirror Lake. In no hurry to get to transition, on instinct, I went to the lakeside to take some photos of the water that would soon be filled with 2000 thrashing swimmers.

The serenity of the water and the fog was a great visual to start the day. The first of many times that the sights of the day would help create a great Ironman racing experience.

Swim

As nice as a calm trip to transition was, the race had to start. Back to reality.

I usually dread the Ironman swim. I am not a great swimmer, I don't really have the time to devote getting much better (I use any extra time on the bike), and have come to believe that the crowded 2000-athlete swims create so much congestion that it isn't worth trying to get much better. Typically, I get stuck in the bunch and clobbered.

This year, my fifth swim start in Lake Placid, I told myself I needed to do something completely different. I wanted to avoid the pounding of the swim start, so I went as wide right as possible, standing in the shallow water, waiting for the cannon. Then, when the cannon fired, I did something else different: I waited. I counted to 15, letting the people ahead of me slug it out, then waded into the water and began my swim.

The underwater white line that attaches the buoys together in Lake Placid seduces hundreds of swimmers, who gravitate towards it from the start thinking the line makes their swim shorter and – one would assume – faster. But there's lots of contact in that group, so I consistently stayed far right, knowing I was swimming a bit longer, but actually able to swim, not just defend myself.

Exiting the water after lap 1, the clock read 35 minutes, better than I expected or deserved. The second lap went just about as well, and I finished the swim in 1 hour, 11 minutes, about the same as I always do in Lake Placid. This was good, and a pleasant surprise. On top of that, I actually enjoyed the swim.

Bike

The Ironman USA bike course is a favorite, and I looked forward to getting on the road and riding. Because this was how the day was going to be – a long training ride day. I had only ridden more than 45 miles once since Ironman Arizona, so while I was well trained to ride the first 56 mile lap, I wasn't sure how the second lap would go.

The two-loop, 56-mile bike course is a beautiful, well designed course filled with great panoramas, tough climbs and thrilling descents. I always drive the bike course the day before a race, in an effort to plan riding strategy. This year, on that pre-race course tour, I took my camera, and in addition to scouting, I tried to capture some of the breathtaking scenery that we'd see on race day.

And there are no shortage of beautiful things to see on the course (see photos). The small lake at mile 8/64 just after the long climb out of town. The screaming, winding descent into Keene amid green forests. The challenge of long climb beginning at mile 44/100 back to town is balanced somewhat by the flowing water and waterfalls that stretch for miles. It's a great bike course to see, let alone ride.

So, knowing this ride might not be my best, I just settled in to ride as best as I could, and to enjoy the scenery. I did feel great on the first lap, finishing it in a fast and fun 21+ mph, or 2:37. The winds picked up on the second lap, as they always seem to do. But they seemed to always be headwinds, even when the course changed direction. On the other hand, I told myself, maybe the truth was that I just wasn't strong enough at this point to remain fast on the second lap of this challenging course.

Whatever it was, I was slowing down. Only a few passed me, so that was a decent sign that I wasn't losing position or time to others. Until . . . the strange mechanical problem.

You check everything on your bike the day before the race. You obsess over everything, you check the tires. Everything. But cleats? After 25 Ironman events, there still was something new that could go wrong.

With more than 20 miles to go, I approached the turnaround at the end of Haselton Road. It's a tight turn, and I prepared to unclip my left shoe for balance. Except I couldn't unclip, my foot just swung wide. I knew the problem right away: two of the three screws holding the cleat to my shoe had fallen out. And it felt like the last cleat was ready to go. Not a good thing when the course's most significant climbs were ahead.

For the next few miles, I rode delicately, trying to figure out if I could climb if the cleat came off altogether. Seeing the bike support team ahead, I pulled over to ask for assistance. After several minutes of scrounging through toolboxes, they found nothing, so just tightened the remaining screw as much as possible. So, several lost minutes, no real fix, unfortunately. It happens. A new lesson: Check everything, and that means Everything.

The rest of the ride continued without event, although slowly, and I pulled into transition with a 5:37 bike ride. Not bad, I was happy. Better than I deserved for my training this year, and good base to build on for upcoming races.

Run

I have run my best Ironman Marathon in Lake Placid (3:26 in 2004) on my way to my best Ironman finish time that year (10:12). But exiting the transition area and heading onto the run course, I knew I would not approach either of those times. Rather than being disappointed, I felt relief, actually. I could simply enjoy the run, if running 26.2 miles is your form of enjoyment.

When you start the marathon in an Ironman, you wonder: how can I possibly run for the next 3-4 hours or more. It seems so far, so long. You keep running along and the first mile marker seems to take forever to show up. Same with the second and the third. Forever.

But soon you fall into a zone, and forget that you started at 7am, forget that you swam 2.4 miles, forget that you rode your toughest 112 miles of the year. You forget all that, and you just keep moving forward accepting what you see, hear and think.

The sights on the run, as on the bike course, could be awesome, especially the Olympic Training Ski Jumps, towering over the turn that marks the approximate 3/8/16/21 mile marks (see photos). The day before, I had gone to watch a ski jump competition there. The jumpers literally threw themselves off the side of the mountain, flying up to 100 meters, seemingly effortlessly, without fear.

The run course heads through trees away from the ski jump, and for a few miles, to the turnaround at about 5.5/18.5 miles and back, you really can't see much more than the forest. Then when you emerge, heading back toward town, seeing the ski jumps just makes you smile. Especially the second time around. You know you are close to home, and your day is nearly done.

Finish

The spectators and the racers seemed to be in great spirits, cheering, encouraging, smiling all day. Never more so than when heading back into Lake Placid for the finish. You just couldn't help smiling with them, and to yourself. This had been a good day.

Nearing my 25th Ironman finish line, I reflected on all those previous races. Some had been great, some had been terrible. Some had been hot, some had been in driving, windy rain. Some had been near home, some had been halfway around the world. Some had resulted in qualifying for Kona. Some had been in Kona.

Then there was this finish. The most important part of this finish was that by being the 25th one, it was special. It wasn't about Kona, it wasn't about best times, it wasn't about pressure. It was about opening my eyes, ears and heart to all that was part of the event, enjoying it, getting the most out of it, and doing pretty well along the way.

Ironman USA Lake Placid, New York, July 2007

I had a single, simple goal for my 2007 Ironman USA Lake Placid, my 28th Ironman race: to reach the finish without wondering why I put myself through the torture of Ironman one more time.

In the past, I'd raced for personal bests, I'd raced for Kona, I'd raced to push myself harder than ever before. Not this time.

For 11 hours and 30 minutes at the 2007 Ironman in Lake Placid, I delivered a reasonably fast race (considering my limited training window), and literally made it to the end pain-free, without aches, without struggle, without giving up.

In five previous races in Lake Placid, I've been faster and I've been slower. But I'd never enjoyed it as much as I did in 2007.

It was the easiest Ironman I've ever raced. On one of the harder Ironman courses in the world. How?

Fifteen months earlier, during the Ironman Arizona 2006 race, I realized I had had enough. I was burned out. It hurt too much. It didn't seem worth it. It didn't seem fun anymore. I liked the training, not the competitive racing.

So I stopped.

I skipped what had been my annual favorite triathlons – IM Lake Placid, IM Wisconsin, and Chicago Triathlon – without a tinge of regret. I was on the sidelines in Wisconsin and Chicago, observing and shooting photos, but not wishing I was on the course.

I had signed up for the 2007 Ironman Lake Placid race, like everyone else, the day after the 2006 event, just in case I wanted to race. For most of 2007, I planned on skipping it.

Then in early June 2007, just seven weeks before Ironman Lake Placid, I changed my mind. Having raced there five previous times, I really liked the Lake Placid race, and I was beginning to get the itch to return.

But when I decided to race, I promised myself this time it would be different. New Rule: If it's not fun, it's not worth doing.

I wanted to race Lake Placid without spending a second wishing I was not on the course, without a moment asking 'why do I do this to myself', without those seemingly unending times of struggle and pain, without giving up.

With seven weeks until the race, I needed to build endurance and speed quickly. But I applied the same approach to my training: when it stops being fun, stop doing it. So I kept it simple, did what I wanted to do.

Take a look at my 2007 Training Plans to examine my training over the seven weeks prior to Ironman USA Lake Placid. By the time I reached the week before the race, I was well short of my usual Ironman racing peak condition, but I was happy where I was.

I knew when I arrived in the transition area on race morning, I'd be prepared to have a great day of endurance. All I wanted to do on race day was to enjoy swimming a smooth 2.4 miles, riding 112 miles in the beautiful Adirondacks, and run a steady 26.2 miles, consistently, to a solid finish.

Swim

Race morning was chilly but calm as the sun rose over the mist rising off of the glass-smooth Mirror Lake. More than 2200 racers made their way to the swim start, and from what I can tell, all got in the water before the gun.

I had entered the water at about 6:45pm, and swam to the far side of the start area. Once there, I found a rock to rest upon, as I looked back over the growing field. Soon, there was little room for many of the swimmers, especially just to the right of the starting line.

This is where I knew hundreds of swimmers were poised to pounce on the most direct path in the water -- along a thin white line, just below the water's surface, that stretched from buoy to buoy. I could just imagine the pounding that many of them were about to suffer (which was later confirmed), while I was happy to remain as far away as possible.

When the cannon fired at 7am, I eased into swimming position, and started slowly. I wasn't sure what to expect. I hadn't been in the water to swim, really, since April 2006. You heard right.

I really don't like swimming, so I stayed out of the water, completely, since Ironman Arizona. I had been using the Vasa Ergometer for cross-training in winter 2007, and really enjoyed that land-based workout, so that became my swim training. So I had several 1 to 2 mile 'swim' sessions under my belt before getting into the water, but I was unsure about how the land-based training might translate.

To my happy surprise, I felt great in the water. The motion on the Vasa felt identical in the water, with a natural motion that was most comfortable. Consistent with my goal of taking it easy in the water, I was not interested in setting any swim time-trial records. I just wanted to get through the swim with nearly 100% of my energy intact for the bike and run.

My first quarter of the swim, from the start to the far end of Mirror Lake, took place on the outer fringes of the pack. I did not want to get mixed up in any contact, so when in doubt, I moved to the outside. I sacrificed some benefits of drafting, but felt fresher mentally and physically.

The water was still somewhat frothy from all the swimmers, and I really could not see the buoys or course direction in those first 15 to 20 minutes. So I just spotted relative to other swimmers near me. As long as I was near others, I assumed they were headed the correct direction, and I followed them.

The pack seemed to thin out after the first turnaround, and even though I was only trying to stay near the outside swimmers, soon I was surprised to find myself swimming on the line, buoy to buoy. Soon, I could hear the voice of the race announcer, which meant we were nearing the end of the first lap. Taking stock as I entered the second lap, I felt excellent, if still not fast. That was fine with me.

The second lap seemed faster and smoother than the first. Time passed quickly, despite a distinctly slower lap time that the clock revealed when I got out of the water at the end of the 2.4 mile swim. I realized time was flying while I was having fun. That was the goal.

Bike

The Ironman USA Lake Placid bike course is one of my favorite on the Ironman circuit. As I told some people before the race, 'the course can kick you, and you can kick the course.' Meaning: this is a difficult bike course in many ways, but there are ways to turn the challenges to your advantage, gaining some speed from the climbs that can take it away from you.

The first 14 miles to Keene Valley are, I believe, quite a perfect way to start a hilly bike course. The first miles include several climbs that force you to settle into a steady rhythm while discouraging any attempts to hammer too early. Your leg muscles are warmed up with inclines followed by lesser declines allowing increased cadence and higher speed. After seven miles, the fun begins, and the screaming downhills begin. For the next few minutes, I, and others around me, flew down to Keene Valley under blue skies, no wind and perfect conditions.

The next 10 flat miles to the town of Jay flew by, and then we took the left turn toward Wilmington. The next few miles featured longer, steadier climbs, and I concentrated on pedaling in complete circles, while keeping my breathing easy and constant. It was working. I could hear others around me gasping a little, and knew they were struggling already.

This reminded me that I did not want to get to that point anywhere on the bike course. I would need to maintain a pace that did not lead me to the point of huffing and puffing.

This was my sixth time racing Ironman Lake Placid, but as I rode the 14-mile out and back on Haselton Road in Wilmington, I could have sworn that it was easier, with less challenging small hills, than I had remembered. What was really happening: I was hammering less, and more prepared to take this section comfortably. This was good.

Exiting Haselton Road, the course heads directly to the base of Whiteface Mountain, to the part on the elevation chart that scares most athletes. It looks like it goes straight up for 10 miles. In reality, it's a steady escalation, with periods of relief, but it is ultimately unrelenting. I rode through this section relaxed, not hammering, not worried about speed.

In fact, my bike computer had not been working at all, so I had no idea how fast I had been riding. I was fine with that. Less to worry about, the pressure to go fast, which I tend to apply to myself, was removed.

Like the Haselton section, the climb back into Lake Placid to complete the first 56 mile lap seemed shorter and easier than I had remembered. Even the final four back-to-back climbs -- nicknamed Baby, Brother, Mama and Papa Bear -- seemed inconsequential enough for me to wonder if the course had skipped one or two of them.

Again, time and climbs flying while riding steady and having fun. The difference between this ride and what I had done in the past: I had not been riding at my limit, and I was riding within the range of my training.

I had done winter training on my CompuTrainer, but my outdoor training rides had been lacking. That needed to change. I quickly jumped to regular 40 and 50 mile weekday rides, and my longest ride before Lake Placid was 63 miles.

While I had raced Lake Placid in the past on a base of weekly 100-mile rides, I still had confidence I knew the course well enough to take my limited training to 112 miles without difficulty.

Entering Lap 2, I knew I would soon reach the point marking my longest ride since April 2006. The wind had picked up, and became a noticeable challenge. In the past when I had encountered strong wind on an Ironman course, from Roth Germany to Penticton Canada, I had internally cursed at it, and tried to force myself through it.

This time, I simply accepted that it would slow me -- and everyone nearby -- down a mile per hour or two. I stuck to the plan that had been working so far: steady circular pedaling, smooth cadence, never pushing the breathing. I was also staying on top of salt tabs, taking one every 90 minutes. All of this was helping.

Nearing the 70 mile point, I began to feel the concern that always creeps up on me at that stage of the ride. For some reason, I have often bonked around the 70-mile mark, but have often found a way to get out of it over the next 30 miles, though tended to not be pleasant.

This time, I passed through 70, then 80, then 90, and even 100 miles feeling great. At 100 miles, the Lake Placid course presents the return climb to Lake Placid, typically a stretch of screaming quads, grimacing, and some choice swear words.

To my complete amazement, I felt like a Tour de France rider, spinning on those final miles as comfortably as possible at that point in the race. Reaching the transition area with what turned out to be a 5:50 bike split (not my fastest on the course, not my slowest either), it was clear that sticking to a simple no-hammer, ride within my comfort zone approach was working.

Could I keep it up on the run?

Run

I had been running marathons consistently, though not fast, even after I stopped racing in triathlons. I have always been a runner first, and I do enjoy running in triathlon. But in running competition and in most Ironmans, I had always been driven to push as hard as possible, to fight through the pain to achieve the best time possible.

Then I was introduced to a new way of experiencing long-distance running by Dean Karnazes.

Last year, Dean, who's a stunt-ultramarathoner and very nice guy, toured the country running 50 marathons in 50 states in 50 days. I joined him on three of those occasions, in Des Moines, Arizona, and Chicago. To make it through the journey, he ran the daily marathons casually, at about a 4-hour pace, most of the time with a smile on his face, and with time to converse with whichever runner was at his shoulder.

I had been used to running at speed, trying to get from A to B as fast as possible, but when running with Dean, this was, of course, out of the question. And it was fun. Really fun. It was a new way of running, just to enjoy it.

I took this philosophy to my run training. Time and distance were what I concentrated on, not speed. This was a welcome break from my running approach since I had begun running in 1994.

In each of my five previous races in Lake Placid, I remember taking my first steps onto the run course fairly gingerly, as my strained quads protested the new running motion. It had taken me a while to get used to running, and even then, most of the marathon would be run in various stages of discomfort, from cramping to forced walking.

This time, as on the bike, I was most happy to start running with what felt like almost completely fresh legs. In the first mile, I ran up the sharp incline just past the first aid station, a first for me. I had also skipped the aid station entirely, while in the past, it had been a welcome oasis to load up on Gatorade and Cola.

I just kept going as if I was running those marathons with Dean. Not in any hurry, not too slowly, either. It was what enough spectators called 'good pace!' for me to believe that it was actually true.

Following the course past the Olympic Ski Jumps, to the River Road turnaround, and back into Lake Placid, it all felt great. I settled into a rhythm of stopping at every other aid station for two cups of cola with ice, allowing myself to walk a few steps while drinking. I also allowed myself to power walk the inclines, to help keep my breathing under control.

By the time I neared the Olympic Oval containing the finish line, and saw the arrow pointing to 'Lap 2', I didn't feel the usual dread of having to run the loop again. This was beginning to feel like a long training run at home, and I really didn't want it to end.

The sun was heading to the west and the air was cooling slightly. I headed out to the ski jumps and River Road, not even counting the miles. When I'm feeling stressed in races, I start looking ahead, looking for mile markers telling me I'm that much closer to the finish. This time, I felt no such need for it to be over.

As I returned to Lake Placid for the final time, my pace was about the same as it had been when I started. I still felt good. I realized that I had made it through the day with no more pain or struggle than on any training day in the previous seven weeks.

During that training time, I sought increasing distance and speed, but always at a relatively easy level of effort. The data in my training plans shows that I was able to achieve it. But the best part was that I was able to bring that conditioning from training at home to the course of Ironman Lake Placid.

Rounding the final curve on the Olympic Oval, the finish line came into view. The clock read 11:30:xx, a better Ironman time than I had seen in two years. And more importantly, a great time considering I had just completed what I considered to be my easiest Ironman ever.

I crossed the finish line not with a collapse of relief, but with a smile on the outside, and delight on the inside. The goal had been met: Ironman was fun once again, and I was eager to do it again. And I will.

Bike Course Tips: Riding a 5:36 Split

Ironman Lake Placid Bike Course: Everything You Need to Know

The Ironman USA Bike course is one of the most beautiful, but also one of the toughest 112-mile Ironman rides you'll ever experience. While the course features exceptional scenery and some very generous downhill sections, the course can demoralize and defeat riders on the last 10 miles of each lap.

In short, you can have a great ride on the first three sections, but you'll give it all back on your way past Whiteface to transition. So pay attention.

With a carefully constructed riding strategy, you can ride with strength through the roughest sections, complete the course with a solid bike split, and be ready to begin your marathon with energy to spare.

That's what's presented here, in the form of a 5:36:12 bike split I rode in one of my six races at Ironman Lake Placid. I'll break the course down into sections, describe what you can expect in each one, and provide actual splits to help guide your riding strategy.

So let's get down to business. Here's everything you need to know about the Ironman Lake Placid Bike course.

For starters, the key thing is to break the course down into manageable sections. In each lap, there are four clearly defined segments to consider (distances are approximate):

1. From T1 to Keene: 14 miles
2. From Keene to Jay to Wilmington: 15 miles
3. The Haselton Road out-and-back: 14 miles
4. Whiteface Mountain climb to transition: 13 miles

As we go through these segments, it's important to consider the parameters: my complete split was 5:36:12, or about 20 miles per hour overall. I covered the first 56-mile lap in 2:44:00, or 20.5 mph. I slowed on the second lap to 2:52:12, or 19.5 mph.

Lap 1	Distance	Split	Time/mile	mph
Keene	14.0	0:34:30	0:02:28	24.3
Hasleton	15.0	0:44:00	0:02:56	20.5
Out/back	14.0	0:38:30	0:02:45	21.8
T2	13.0	0:47:00	0:03:37	16.6
	56.0	2:44:00	0:02:56	20.5

Lap 2	Distance	Split	Time/mile	mph
Keene	14.0	0:36:14	0:02:35	23.2
Hasleton	15.0	0:45:09	0:03:01	19.9
Out/back	14.0	0:41:29	0:02:58	20.2
T2	13.0	0:49:21	0:03:48	15.8
	56.0	2:52:12	0:03:05	19.5

| Total | 112.0 | 5:36:12 | 0:03:00 | 20.0 |

The data examples, e.g., noting that it takes 20 minutes to climb from miles 3 to 8, are in this context. These are my actual times; yours may well vary. So view my data as a relative benchmark. If you hope to ride a 6-hour split, for example, adjust my data to meet your expectations.

Segment 1: Transition to Keene – 14 miles

This first segment on the bike course is a mixed bag of uphills and downhills, with an emphasis on the downhill: a screaming descent to Keene. This segment is best seen as an additional four sections.

Miles 1 to 2 -- T1 to Ski Jumps. Walk your bike through the transition area and do not mount it until you cross the official line in the parking lot on the south side of Lake Placid High School.

Once you clip into the pedals, you'll immediately roll down a steep decline from School St. to Colden Ave. You'll be excited to start, but be very careful here. There's a sharp left turn at the base of Colden, taking you onto Route 73. Go too fast at the start, and you'll wind up crashing into hay bales before you've gone 200 meters.

As you get going on Route 73, take some time to make sure you're set on the bike. Nutrition in place, pull up arm warmers if you've got them, straighten the sunglasses, just settle in. Without trying to, you'll ride fast.

It's less than six minutes out of town, at 21.8 mph, and then you reach the ski jumps.

Miles 3 to 7– High Peaks These miles are a series of steady, manageable ascents of 150 meters or so, overall. Don't push the pace here. Find a steady rhythm in a good gear, and plan on riding for 18 minutes or so. This climb is actually a good thing to settle all riders down. Few feel like passing, and you shouldn't either.

You'll know this section is almost over when you see a sign for the Mt. Van Hovenberg Recreation Area on your right. Just ahead will be one gentler incline. Consider this segment of 5 miles as a warm-up. And not a fast one -- I finish it at an average speed of 15mph.

Miles 8 to 10 – Cascade Lakes. At about the 8-mile point, you'll enter a two-mile section of slight rollers that pass the scenic Upper Cascade Lakes on your right.

Now's the time to hammer a little. Let gravity work for you -- pedal hard on the slight downhill grades and you can pick up speed and start passing riders. I cover this part in 5 minutes at 24.0mph.

When you reach Lower Cascade Lake, also to your right, you, yourself, are about to cascade downhill at a frightening rate.

Miles 10 to 14 – The Screaming Descent. These are the miles you've been hearing about and looking forward to: the screaming descent to Keene. It's the fastest 6 minutes you'll ever experience on an Ironman course, and that equates to 40mph.

And I ride this part cautiously. Riders will pass you going even faster. I don't see the risks of riding 50mph as worth saving a few seconds.

If the weather is wet and/or windy, be careful, stay under control. Accidents on this stretch could be very nasty, what with all the downward momentum.

Sometimes riders experience a shaking of the front wheel, at high speed, and it's hard to control. To avoid this, try to keep your bike stable by hugging the frame with your knees on the way down.

Be realistic in knowing that this descent will not make much of a difference in your overall bike split. If you ride it 80mph, you save only three minutes. So be safe, enjoy it, and it's on to the next major segment.

Adding it up from the start, I cover these first 14 miles at 24.3 mph overall, without working too hard.

Segment 2: Keene to Wilmington – 15 miles

Segment 2 includes the relatively flat and fast 10 miles from Keene through Upper Jay to the adjacent town of Jay, followed by a generally uphill stretch of five miles from Jay to Wilmington.

Miles 15 to 24 -- Keene to Jay. This segment of eleven miles may be the longest, easiest stretch on the course , but you have to work a little. You can start riding at speed here, but, again, don't hammer. We're trying to be smart, and you need to keep yourself in check.

You'll enjoy the scenery of rocky streams for much of your ride from Keene to the town of Jay, as the course meanders gently right and left, through dense wooded passages and wide open spaces.

Road signs will give you a sense of where you are: you'll reach Upper Jay after about the 20 mile marker, and four more miles to Jay.

Ride these miles fast, feel free to push it a little. A little. Even while not hammering much, I ride these 10 miles to Jay at around 22 miles per hour.

Miles 25 to 29 -- Jay to Wilmington. When you enter Jay, you'll take a hard right turn onto Route 86 toward Wilmington. From there it's a 5 mile trip to Haselton Road. As you approach the turn, get into an easy gear, because you'll need it for the 1-mile climb. Like the initial climb on the course, settle in here, and just spin.

Once over the top of this 1-mile climb, the next four miles are rolling and fun, but still challenging. On balance, you'll be mostly climbing as Whiteface Mountain begins to come into view on the horizon, to your left.

I complete these 5 miles in 17 minutes, 17.6 mph. It seems slow, but others will be riding slower. You can use these miles to your advantage.

Make sure to get the most of the declines. Begin to pedal hard as you crest the hills here, and hammer on the way down. You'll pass many riders this way. They'll coast; you'll pass easily without working too much harder. Make the hills work for you.

And my totals for this second segment – Keene to Jay to Haselton Road -- 14 miles, 21.6mph. Remember: the overall speed on this segment could be slower, unless you take advantage of the declines on the last few miles.

Average speed from the start through 29 miles: about 22mph. Fast, but still in control.

Arriving in Wilmington, you'll be zooming at a fast clip toward the hard right turn onto Haselton Road. You'll have to be careful on the turn because you'll only have one lane; the other lane is occupied by riders coming the other way. Accidents do happen at this turn. Sit up, apply the brakes, and be careful.

Segment 3: Haselton Road Out-and-Back -- 14 miles

The next fourteen miles are, generally, a fast and fun ride. It's also unique from the rest of the bike course, with nearly the entire distance under the share of tall trees. I remember this whole section as being the greenest part of the course. Really nice, visually.

Miles 30 to 36. This can be another fast segment. The miles are gently rolling, for the most part. Again, get the most out of the rollers by pedaling over the top and hammering down the other side.

Make gravity work for you. That's how you'll continue to ride faster here, and elsewhere on the course. Take the forward momentum, lock into a big gear and go. This tactic may make the difference between getting a Kona slot or not. Seriously.

The course elevation map says otherwise, but I always feel the outbound portion declines overall. At least it seems to favor speed most of the time. But things to change in the last mile before the turnaround, when you do climb about 150 meters.

You'll know you're approaching the turnaround as the volume of riders heading the other way will grow. It may seem like hundreds pass you on their way back, and it may feel very frustrating. Don't let it get to you.

If you're riding smart, you'll probably pass one or two hundred on the second lap. Seriously. Let them crush the first lap; many of them will suffer for it on the next 56 miles. You won't.

Miles 37 to 43. When you get to the turnaround, load up on nutrition and liquids. While heading back on the return 7 miles, you want to be fueling and preparing for the last 10 miles of the first lap.

Also, soon after you pass the 40-mile marker, you'll have a very taxing climb, perhaps the steepest on the course. When you get there, you'll know it. Don't panic. Get in your easiest gear, and just pedal smoothly and consistently.

I ride the 14 mile out-and-back on Haselton Road in 38 minutes, an average speed of 22mph. I'm usually pretty consistent: 19 minutes out, 19 minutes back. Again, the difference is how I work the descents. A little extra effort pays dividends with a lot of speed.

At this point on the course, roughly 43 miles have gone by in about 2 hours, at an average speed of 21.8mph.

What was I saying earlier about Lake Placid being the toughest course? Seems pretty easy through 43 miles. That's because . . .

Segment 4: to Whiteface Mountain and T2 – 13 miles

The large orange 'Road Closed' sign is marks the beginning of the end. Everything changes when you pass the orange sign. Buckle up, time to face the beast.

Mile 44. Mercifully, the first mile or so is relatively flat, giving you time to hydrate, relax, and get ready to climb.

If there's any good news to share, it's that the 300 meter overall elevation gain is spread out over the next 10 miles, and therefore doesn't slam you too hard at any one place.

You will work your way upwards, but it'll have a sort of switchback feel, without switching back. It's more like a ½ mile incline, ¼ slight descent, and the like. Over and over.

You will see your average speed plunge. It just will. You'll have to be mentally ready to give back a lot of the speed you had through 43 miles. But so will everyone else. And those who ride these final miles strategically will be that much closer to a great bike split.

Miles 45 to 48. You may be hardest hit in the beginning. I ride miles 45 to 48 at an average of 15mph. You just don't want to fight it too much. It's too early. Sit up in the saddle, get out of the aero bars, try to relax and just spin as consistently as you can.

Miles 49 to 52. Things should get better for you here. You're still working hard, but you'll have gotten used to the grind. I gain speed here, riding it a couple notches better, at 17mph.

Miles 53 to 56. You've heard about the Bears, no doubt. Baby, Mama and Papa Bear. These are the names given the final, challenging climbs to face before the lap is over. Unless time has worn away the paint, you'll spot the name of the next Bear before you get there. You will see it because you will be looking down much of the time, at that point. You'll be digging for everything you've got as you slowly spin toward the finish.

The lesson you've hopefully learned by now is that going uphill offers a significant opportunity to gain speed and pass people on the other side. The Bears each make you work long and hard, but when you crest the top, each time, pedal hard and hammer down the other side.

Everyone else will be gliding. You'll want to glide. Don't. This is easy speed, easy chances to move yourself higher in the race standings.

Still, you will be gasping for air one way or the other when you make what will be an extremely slow right turn from Route 86 onto Northwood Rd. You've made it at that point, really. The next mile back into town is a fast one as the adrenaline kicks in.

I ride miles 53 to 56 at an average of about 18 miles per hour. These miles are perhaps the most daunting in terms of work as well as how late in the race they hit you. But you can hit back, and you can ride well. Getting to 18.5 proves it. That's the difference a well-constructed riding strategy can make.

You'll know you've made it through one of the toughest Ironman Bike courses in the world. You'll hear the cheer of the crowd as you near the transition area, and it will bring a smile.

Except for one thing: you've got to do it again.

At the end of lap 1, with 56 miles complete, I was at 2:44:00, an average of 20.5mph. A good start, but I've never found it easy to repeat it.

Twice the Fun: Lap 2

Lap 2 for me was twelve minutes longer, 2:56:12, averaging 19.5 mph. Shoot for that. Map a strategy for lap 2 that has you riding about 5% slower. Total for 112 miles: 5:36:12, just about 20mph.

The second lap feels relentless, especially the final 13 miles. It's these last 13 miles that makes Ironman Lake Placid one of the toughest out there.

When you're at 100 miles complete, and you're climbing, you'll know what it's like in the Tour de France: not the least bit easy, but worth it in the end.

It's a fantastic feeling to finish 112 miles in Lake Placid, and you'll feel the rush of excitement as you head into T2 to drop off your bike.

If you've ridden well, according to your race strategy, you'll have plenty left over to run a sub-4 marathon. Yes, you will.

IM LP Preparation and Racing Strategies
- Training Plan Strategy 2002
- Detailed Day-by-Day Training Plan 2002
- Everything Else You Need to Know

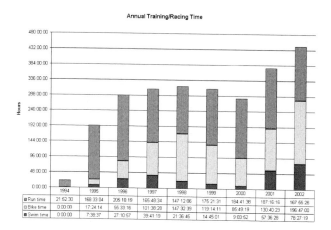

Annual Training/Racing Time

	1994	1995	1996	1997	1998	1999	2000	2001	2002
☒ Run time	21:52:30	168:33:04	205:10:19	165:48:34	147:12:06	175:21:31	184:41:38	187:16:16	167:55:26
☐ Bike time	0:00:00	17:24:14	55:33:16	101:38:28	147:32:39	119:14:11	85:49:19	130:40:23	196:47:00
■ Swim time	0:00:00	7:38:37	27:10:57	39:41:19	21:36:45	14:45:01	9:03:52	57:36:28	78:27:19

Training Plan Strategy 2002

After several plateau racing performance years, 2002 was a breakthrough year, including a 2:54 Boston Marathon and qualifying for Kona 2002 and 2003. Looking at my 2002 training log, it's easy to see the changes I made in training to achieve this new level of performance.

First, some background, for perspective. As of 2002, I was 42 years old, married 18 years with four kids, and had a busy job as a marketing/strategy executive. I never had – and will never have – the kind of hours available that people tend to put in to be their best at Ironman racing. So I had to make do. My program may not be right for everybody, but it worked for me.

From 1997 to 2000, I pretty much proved that if I trained an average of 6 hours per week – roughly 1 hour swimming, 2.5 hours biking, 2.5 hours running -- I could complete Ironman triathlons in the 11 to 12 hour range. In fact, I completed eleven of them. It was great to get the finisher's medals, but I wasn't progressing.

In 2001, I stepped up the volume, averaging about 7.25 hours training, with a little more emphasis on cycling, and began to close the Kona qualification gap. 2001 ended with 57 hours and 103 miles swimming; 130 hours and 2463 miles cycling; and 187 hours and 1522 miles running.

Training Summary 1997 to 2002: Core Data

Swim, Bike, Run

	1997	1998	1999	2000	2001	2002
Miles	3,056.5	3,803.3	3,502.2	2,928.4	4,089.2	5,324.8
Time	307:08:21	316:21:30	309:20:43	279:34:49	375:33:07	443:09:45
Sessions	282	289	261	259	366	390
Distance/Session	10.8	13.2	13.4	11.3	11.2	13.65
Time/session	1:05:21	1:05:41	1:11:07	1:04:46	1:01:34	1:08:11
Time/mile	06:02	04:59	05:18	05:44	05:31	04:59.6
Time/week	5:54:23	6:05:02	5:56:56	5:22:36	7:12:09	8:31:20

Swim

	1997	1998	1999	2000	2001	2002
Miles	68.9	38.2	27.4	15.3	103.5	146.3
Time	39:41:19	21:36:45	14:45:01	9:03:52	57:36:28	78:27:19
Sessions	59	36	26	13	96	121
Distance/Session	1.2	1.1	1.1	1.2	1.1	1.21
Time/session	0:40:22	0:36:01	0:34:02	0:41:50	0:36:00	0:38:54
Time/mile	34:32	0:33:57	0:32:17	0:35:32	0:33:24	32:10.2

Bike

	1997	1998	1999	2000	2001	2002
Miles	1,781.5	2,667.9	2,276.1	1,525.8	2,463.6	3,830.8
Time	101:38:28	147:32:39	119:14:11	85:49:19	130:40:23	196:47:00
Sessions	78	120	101	70	107	129
Distance/Session	22.8	22.2	22.5	21.8	23.0	29.70
Time/session	1:18:11	1:13:46	1:10:50	1:13:34	1:13:16	1:31:32
Time/mile	03:25	03:19	03:09	03:22	03:11	03:04.9

Run

	1997	1998	1999	2000	2001	2002
Miles	1,206.0	1,097.2	1,198.7	1,387.3	1,522.1	1,347.7
Time	165:48:34	147:12:06	175:21:31	184:41:38	187:16:16	167:55:26
Sessions	145	133	134	176	163	140
Distance/Session	8.3	8.2	8.9	7.9	9.3	9.63
Time/session	1:08:37	1:06:24	1:18:31	1:02:58	1:08:56	1:11:58
Time/mile	08:15	0:08:03	0:08:47	0:07:59	0:07:23	07:28.6

In November 2001 at Ironman Florida, I broke the 11-hour barrier to finish in 10:40. This was 40 minutes from a Kona slot, but it was closer than I had ever been before.

I decided that to shave enough time to qualify for Kona 2002, I needed to redouble my effort on cycling, and run less, but faster. I also needed to achieve a better balance of training, timing and equipment.

By year-end 2002, I had increased swimming by 41% to 78 hours and 146 miles; biking by 55% to 196 hours and 3830 miles, and had cut back my running by 11% to 167 hours and 1347 miles.

In an average week in 2002, I swam 90 minutes, biked 3.75 hours for 73 miles, and ran 3.15 hours and 26 miles. This translated to adding an average of 1.25 hours per week compared with 2001, for a total of 8.5 hours per week.

Training Summary 1997-2002: Annual Changes

Swim, Bike, Run

	1998	1999	2000	2001	2002
Miles	24%	-8%	-16%	40%	30%
Time	3%	-2%	-10%	34%	18%
Sessions	2%	-10%	-1%	41%	7%
Distance/Session	21%	2%	-16%	-1%	22%
Time/session	1%	8%	-9%	-5%	11%
Time/mile	-17%	6%	8%	-4%	-9%
Time/week	3%	-2%	-10%	34%	18%

Swim

	1998	1999	2000	2001	2002
Miles	-45%	-28%	-44%	576%	41%
Time	-46%	-32%	-39%	536%	36%
Sessions	-39%	-28%	-50%	638%	26%
Distance/Session	-9%	-1%	12%	-8%	12%
Time/session	-11%	-6%	23%	-14%	8%
Time/mile	-2%	-5%	10%	-6%	-4%
Time/week	-46%	-32%	-39%	536%	36%

Bike

	1998	1999	2000	2001	2002
Miles	50%	-15%	-33%	61%	55%
Time	45%	-19%	-28%	52%	51%
Sessions	54%	-16%	-31%	53%	21%
Distance/Session	-3%	1%	-3%	6%	29%
Time/session	-6%	-4%	4%	0%	25%
Time/mile	-3%	-5%	7%	-6%	-3%
Time/week	45%	-19%	-28%	52%	51%

Run

	1998	1999	2000	2001	2002
Miles	-9%	9%	16%	10%	-11%
Time	-11%	19%	5%	1%	-10%
Sessions	-8%	1%	31%	-7%	-14%
Distance/Session	-1%	8%	-12%	18%	3%
Time/session	-3%	18%	-20%	9%	4%
Time/mile	-2%	9%	-9%	-8%	1%
Time/week	-11%	19%	5%	1%	-10%

Periodization

My weekly training varied to appropriately build up to each major race, with a generally decent taper beforehand (though I tend to taper less than most), and a reasonable recovery period afterwards. This is obvious from looking at the chart of my weekly training time.

The builds to each major event -- Ironman New Zealand in week 9, Ironman USA in week 31, Ironman Wisconsin in week 38, then Ironman Hawaii in week 42 -- are pretty clear in the chart.

A few things are notable particularly the 24 week build to my qualifying race in Lake Placid. After recovering from Ironman New Zealand briefly, I entered marathon season in April (Boston) and May (Mad City Marathon), but wrapped additional cycling in most weeks, to build from 7-hour training weeks to 12 hour training weeks by June. You can also see how the running receded, making way for more cycling time in early summer. Also, I undertook a very real two-week taper just before Ironman USA, my first one ever. And it paid dividends.

2002 Weekly Training Mix: Time

Weekly Time

Sum of Time	Type			
Week	Bike	Run	Swim	Grand Total
1	3:12:26	1:55:00	3:00:47	8:08:13
2	9:44:55	2:41:58	0:59:59	13:26:52
3	4:32:42	1:37:47	3:02:44	9:13:13
4	6:15:00	5:33:03	3:56:08	15:44:11
5	3:30:00	0:40:00	1:27:16	5:37:16
6	4:00:00	5:35:22	3:27:57	13:03:19
7	1:30:00	4:20:11	2:02:11	7:52:22
8	4:51:00	1:34:47	3:02:39	9:28:26
9	6:34:36	4:22:44	1:09:42	12:07:02
10	0:30:00	1:40:20	1:33:47	3:44:07
11	1:00:00	3:14:08	1:04:49	5:18:57
12		4:42:58	1:02:02	5:45:00
13		8:01:56	2:31:00	10:32:56
14	2:32:30	6:15:24	1:41:33	10:29:27
15	0:59:00	4:47:15	1:32:04	7:18:19
16	2:53:00	3:54:27	1:36:48	8:24:15
17	6:10:00		1:32:31	7:42:31
18	3:08:22	4:11:28	1:35:07	8:54:57
19	3:02:24	5:15:57	2:16:23	10:34:44
20	5:48:02	3:33:13	3:02:00	12:23:15
21	1:59:05	3:04:20	0:31:54	5:35:19
22	5:00:50	3:27:36	1:09:35	9:38:01
23	7:38:03	1:27:42	3:19:13	12:24:58
24	6:32:58	2:29:50	1:44:35	10:47:23
25	7:57:24	3:24:29	0:20:29	11:42:22
26	3:46:40	5:01:34	2:38:08	11:26:22
27	10:07:17	2:57:04	0:43:44	13:48:05
28	6:46:37	2:49:06	2:32:53	12:08:36
29	3:19:24	3:15:08	0:41:02	7:15:34
30	3:51:50	1:05:46	0:44:47	5:42:23
31	9:42:10	4:34:25	1:31:20	15:47:55
32	4:53:27	1:54:01	2:11:00	8:58:28
33	3:36:42	5:46:02	1:33:25	10:56:09
34	5:09:00	3:10:06	2:30:21	10:49:27
35		1:47:08	0:34:06	2:21:14
36	3:39:45	1:06:42	1:34:12	6:20:39
37	1:40:20	2:28:02	0:39:53	4:48:15
38	7:14:15	3:36:16	2:07:39	12:58:10
39	2:11:18	3:15:45	1:33:30	7:00:33
40	6:26:55	1:39:33	0:15:10	8:21:38
41	3:01:48	2:02:38	1:01:20	6:05:46
42	6:01:54	6:55:46	1:33:41	14:31:21
43		0:45:32		0:45:32
44	0:30:00	0:27:08	0:51:22	1:48:30
45		1:06:01	0:57:40	2:03:41
46	1:32:36	3:31:48		5:04:24
47	2:08:36	1:00:46	0:29:44	3:39:06
48	2:15:00	5:13:42		7:28:42
49	2:04:20	1:56:57	0:58:00	4:59:17
50	1:50:30	3:17:09	2:01:09	7:08:48
51	2:00:30	1:41:28		3:41:58
52	3:33:49	3:28:48		7:02:37
53		4:09:10		4:09:10
Grand Total	196:47:00	167:55:26	78:27:19	443:09:45

After Ironman USA, my training weeks were less
consistent, as I was listening to my body. When it said
rest, I did. But it appears that the buildup for Ironman
USA held, as I was able to run a 2003 qualifying race
seven weeks later in Wisconsin.

Key Differences

In addition to more training time, I did several things
differently than in previous years.

First, I cycled more than 1500 indoor miles on my
CompuTrainer in the winter months. These sessions
varied from 30 minutes to more than 5 hours, from
strength and speed work to long endurance rides. In
early 2002, I made sure to ride at least 56 miles on
CompuTrainer once per week. The physical and mental
training was awesome. These winter indoor training
miles, utilizing the heart rate, cadence and wattage
feedback, brought me into the spring season strong and
fast.

Second, I did nearly a complete reversal after running
Boston in 2:54 in April. My friend and xtri contributor,

Art Hutchinson, had a thought, and he wasn't kidding:
'you've proven you can run, so why don't you
substitute serious rides for your planned runs, and cut
back your running to basic maintenance.' By years'
end, I was still able to comfortably run a 3:05 Chicago
Marathon, though I was running much than 25 miles
per week in training.

2002 Weekly Training Mix: Distance

Weekly Distance

Sum of Dist	Type				
Week	Bike	Run	Swim	(blank)	Grand Total
1	58.6	14.2	5.4		78.3
2	193.8	23.1	1.8		218.8
3	91.9	12.8	5.5		110.2
4	123.1	46.0	7.4		176.4
5	64.3	4.7	2.7		71.7
6	79.4	42.9	6.4		128.6
7	29.7	35.3	3.7		68.7
8	90.5	12.0	5.5		108.0
9	129.0	32.5	2.4		163.9
10	10.0	13.4	2.8		26.2
11	18.1	27.1	1.9		47.1
12		39.4	1.9		41.3
13		54.0	4.5		58.5
14	48.5	51.4	3.2		103.1
15	20.0	41.7	2.9		64.6
16	51.2	35.3	2.9		89.3
17	115.3		2.8		118.2
18	56.8	32.9	3.0		92.7
19	54.4	44.4	4.3		103.1
20	111.7	26.2	5.6		143.4
21	40.0	27.3	1.0		68.3
22	99.3	29.3	2.2		130.8
23	148.4	11.5	6.5		166.4
24	132.1	22.5	3.3		157.9
25	161.4	28.4	0.7		190.4
26	70.8	40.2	5.1		116.0
27	202.4	25.8	1.4		229.6
28	131.8	24.4	4.8		161.0
29	67.7	26.5	1.3		95.5
30	78.2	9.1	1.3		88.6
31	193.9	34.8	3.1		231.8
32	86.7	16.7	4.0		107.4
33	75.2	49.2	3.0		127.4
34	101.7	26.0	4.8		132.5
35		13.9	1.1		15.0
36	69.0	8.6	2.9		80.5
37	32.9	21.6	1.3		55.8
38	142.6	26.2	4.0		172.8
39	44.3	26.3	2.9		73.5
40	114.5	13.0	0.5		128.0
41	60.3	18.8	1.9		81.0
42	112.0	52.4	2.9		167.3
43		6.0			6.0
44	9.0	3.6	1.6		14.2
45		8.5	1.8		10.3
46	30.0	24.6			54.6
47	45.0	9.1	0.9		55.0
48	46.8	40.3			87.1
49	41.0	13.6	1.8		56.4
50	31.8	24.0	3.7		59.5
51	41.4	13.9			55.3
52	74.4	27.3			101.7
53		35.3			35.3
Grand Total	3830.8	1347.7	146.3		5324.8

Third, I lived on my Softride as soon as it got warm enough to train regularly outside. As much as I would miss running, Art was right, and it is obvious in my training log. Morning runs were skipped in favor of regular 27 mile rides at dawn. My average ride distance increased from 23 miles in 2002 to 29 in 2003.

The increased time in the saddle began to yield dividends, and surprisingly, I wasn't losing my running speed. In fact, I was gaining -- I finished top 4 in a local half marathon in June, with a PR time of 1:22. This is not surprising if you look at my logs over time: I have become a faster runner running fewer miles and spending more time on the bike.

Fourth, for the first time ever, I was able to get through the season without running injury. As a serious overpronator, I've always needed stabilization shoes, but couldn't settle on the right one. In 2002 I found it, and ran 1300 miles on five different pairs of Brooks Trance shoes. In my 2002 training log I tracked how many miles per pair, so I would know when to switch pairs. I've learned through this analysis that I need to switch somewhere around 300 miles to stay injury free.

The best part of a detailed review of the past year's (and even before that) training logs, is that they allow you to decipher what worked, what didn't, what you need to keep, and what you need to change as you launch your assault on the next season.

2002 Training Summary

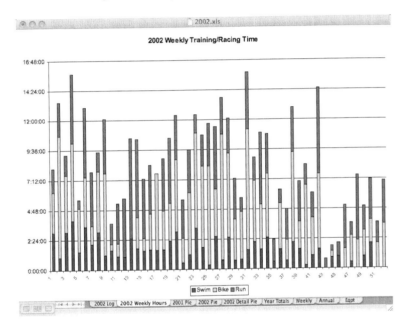

2002 Equipment Summary

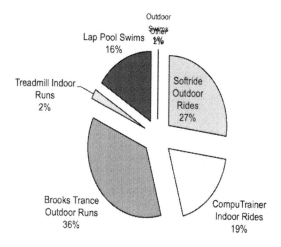

2002 Breakdown of Time, Location and Equipment

	Time	Miles	Workouts
Softride Outdoor Rides	117:28:43	2,295.0	65
CompuTrainer Indoor Rides	79:38:10	1,536.4	65
Brooks Trance Outdoor Runs	155:20:24	1,270.1	119
Treadmill Indoor Runs	9:41:12	55.2	16
Lap Pool Swims	68:35:04	127.7	107
Outdoor Swims	5:21:34	10.5	5
Other	7:04:38	30.0	13
Total	443:09:45	5,324.8	390

Detailed Day by Day Training Plan 2002

Date	Type	Dist	Time	Pace	MPH	Exercise	HR	Watts	Wts	Shoes
1/1	Bike	15.00	0:45:00	03:00.0	20.0	PS1B 3x3xhigh	153	212	xa	CT
1/1	Run	2.63	0:30:00	11:24.4	5.3	P1L7 brick	153			TM
1/2	Swim	1.79	1:00:20	33:42.3	1.8				a	5S
1/2	Bike	23.63	1:25:00	03:35.8	16.7	TDF15/2	150	196		CT
1/3	Swim	1.79	1:00:16	33:40.4	1.8				aPilates	5S
1/4	Bike	20.00	1:02:26	03:07.3	19.2	2x6(+2)x2.5'	148	197	a	CT
1/4	Swim	1.85	1:00:11	32:35.5	1.8	excellent				5S
1/5	Run	11.60	1:25:00	07:19.7	8.2	JP to HP route			aSkating	NXT
1/6	Bike	56.00	2:55:56	03:08.5	19.1	IMNZ lap 1	150	181	xa	CT
1/7									a	
1/8	Swim	1.85	0:59:59	32:29.0	1.8	better			xas	5S
1/8	Bike	25.80	1:15:00	02:54.4	20.6	3x6x2.5' RI 20" 15'w/u	153	214		CT
1/9	Run	9.10	0:59:14	06:30.5	9.2	BT			xa	NXT
1/10	Bike	112.00	5:33:59	02:58.9	20.1	IMNZ	151	197	xa	CT
1/11						60' skating				
1/12	Run	14.02	1:42:44	07:19.7	8.2	JP to HP route				NXT
1/13	Bike	20.10	1:00:00	02:59.1	20.1		150	197	skating	CT
1/14						rest				
1/15	Bike	15.80	0:50:00	03:09.9	19.0	spin	135	175		CT
1/15	Swim	1.85	1:01:08	33:06.4	1.8				xas	5S
1/16	Swim	1.82	1:00:48	33:26.4	1.8				xa	5S
1/17	Swim	1.88	1:00:48	32:25.6	1.9				xas	5S
1/18	Bike	56.00	2:42:42	02:54.3	20.7	IMNZ lap 1	155	216		CT
1/18	Run	1.70	0:17:12	10:07.1	5.9	treadmill brick easy	138			TM
1/19	Run	11.10	1:20:35	07:15.6	8.3	JP route HP				NXT
1/20	Run	8.50	1:00:42	07:08.5	8.4	BG; 40% snow/ice			a	NXT
1/21	Swim	1.99	1:05:15	32:48.7	1.8				xa	5S
1/21	Bike	24.00	1:10:00	02:55.0	20.6	1to6to1 ladder L1 2' RI	150	210		CT
1/21	Run	4.87	0:40:00	08:12.8	7.3	flat treadmill brick	144			NXT2
1/22	Swim	1.85	0:59:08	32:01.4	1.9				xas	5S
1/22	Bike	21.40	1:05:00	03:02.2	19.8	easy CT flat	137	182		CT
1/23	Run	13.10	1:26:34	06:36.5	9.1	HM loop; slick last 3			xa	NXT2
1/24	Swim	1.59	0:50:20	31:38.3	1.9				xa	5S
1/24	Bike	77.65	4:00:00	03:05.4	19.4	IMNZ; struggle through hour 2	140	184		CT
1/25	Run	1.50	0:15:00	10:00.0	6.0	easy brick after ride				NXT2
1/25	Swim	1.93	1:01:25	31:47.5	1.9				xas	5S
1/26	Run	18.00	2:10:47	07:15.9	8.3			153		NXT2
1/27	Bike	27.00	1:30	03:20.0	18.0	estimate; outdoor ride			xa	SR
1/28	Bike	20.54	1:00:00	02:55.3	20.5	4-8-12-8-4 ladder	153	209		CT
1/28	Run	4.66	0:40:00	08:35.0	7.0	brick run	142			TM
1/29	Swim	1.90	1:00:57	32:01.3	1.9	first 1800 in 31:34			as	5S
1/30	Swim	0.82	0:26:19	31:56.6	1.9				xas	5S
1/31						bronchitis, etc.				
2/1						bronchitis, etc.				
2/2	Bike	16.80	1:00:00	03:34.3	16.8	recovery spin	120	130	xa	CT
2/3	Run	9.10	1:10:53	07:47.4	7.7		157			NXT2
2/4	Swim	0.77	0:25:22	33:04.2	1.8					
2/4	Bike	20.00	1:00:00	03:00.0	20.0	15 12 10 ladder	153	203	x	CT
2/5	Swim	1.82	1:00:54	33:29.7	1.8				xas	5S
2/5	Run	4.02	0:45:00	11:11.6	5.4	P1L9 hills 5.4 mph 8-12% grade	160			NXT2
2/6	Swim	1.90	1:01:26	32:16.5	1.9	BT loop			xas	5S
2/6	Run	9.10	1:04:25	07:04.7	8.5					NXT2
2/7	Bike	40.40	2:00:00	02:58.2	20.2	IMNZ loop 40.4	150	197		CT
2/8	Swim	1.88	1:00:15	32:08.0	1.9				xa	5S
2/9	Run	20.65	2:35:04	07:30.6	8.0	HM+				NXT2
2/9	Bike	19.00	1:00:00	03:09.5	19.0	Fort Sheridan outside			xa	SR

Week	Date	Type	Dist	Time	Pace	MPH	Exercise	HR	Watts	Wts	Shoes
7	2/12	Bike	23.00	1:10:00	03:02.6	19.7	10' 5x5' Ladder 3' RI	148	197		CT
7	2/13	Swim	1.85	1:00:12	32:36.0	1.8				s	5S
7	2/13	Run	9.10	1:04:00	07:02.0	8.5					NXT2
7	2/14						exhausted				
7	2/15	Swim	1.88	1:01:59	33:03.5	1.8	exhausted; several breaks			xas	5S
7	2/15	Bike	6.69	0:20:00	02:59.4	20.1	easy spin	144	193		CT
7	2/16	Run	26.20	3:16:11	07:29.3	8.0	easy 1:35/1:41				NXT2
8	2/17	Bike	74.00	4:00:00	03:14.6	18.5	good first hour; then fell off fast	140	175	x	CT
8	2/18	Run	1.50	0:15:00	10:00.0	6.0	brick run				TM
8	2/18	Swim	1.85	1:01:21	33:13.4	1.8	recovery swim			xa	5S
8	2/19	Swim	0.94	0:30:39	32:41.6	1.8	tired			xa	5S
8	2/20	Swim	1.79	1:00:39	33:53.2	1.8	tired			s	5S
8	2/21	Bike	16.50	0:51:00	03:05.5	19.4	10-8-8-4-2-1 session 1,2-1,3 RI 3'			xa	CT
8	2/22						rest				
8	2/23	Run	10.50	1:19:47	07:35.9	7.9	JP, JM for half				NXT2
8	2/23	Swim	0.88	0:30:00	34:03.9	1.8	free form, no tracking			xa	5S
9	2/24	Bike	17.00	0:47:46	02:48.6	21.4	disc wheel test; 20mph gusts				SR
9	2/24	Run	6.30	0:43:26	06:53.7	8.7	brick run			a	NXT2
9	3/2	Swim	2.40	1:09:42	29:02.5	2.1	IMNZ02				
9	3/2	Bike	112.00	5:46:50	03:05.8	19.4	IMNZ02				SR
9	3/2	Run	26.20	3:39:18	08:22.2	7.2	IMNZ02				NXT2
10	3/4	Swim	0.45	0:15:07	33:15.4	1.8	recovery			xa	5S
10	3/5	Swim	0.85	0:28:45	33:44.0	1.8	recovery			xas	5S
10	3/7	Swim	0.60	0:19:55	33:11.7	1.8	recovery			xa	5S
10	3/8	Bike	10.00	0:30:00	03:00.0	20.0	CT spin		130	a	CT
10	3/8	Swim	0.88	0:30:00	34:03.9	1.8	recovery			xa	5S
10	3/8	Run	4.60	0:32:05	06:58.5	8.6	NT				NXT2
10	3/9	Run	8.80	1:08:15	07:45.3	7.7	wind warnings			a	NXT2
11	3/10	Run	8.90	1:07:59	07:38.3	7.9	BG+ strong wind			a	NXT2
11	3/11	Run	9.10	1:03:41	06:59.9	8.6	BT loop			a	NXT2
11	3/12	Bike	18.10	1:00:00	03:18.9	18.1	IMUSA	148	186	a	CT
11	3/13	Swim	0.97	0:32:49	33:58.5	1.8	easy			xa	5S
11	3/14									a	
11	3/15	Swim	0.97	0:32:00	33:07.8	1.8	better			xa	5S
11	3/16	Run	9.10	1:02:28	06:51.9	8.7	BT mixed effort			a	NXT2
12	3/17	Run	13.10	1:24:12	06:25.6	9.3	March Madness 1/2 Marathon				NXT2
12	3/18	Swim	1.88	1:02:02	33:05.1	1.8	mixed			as	5S
12	3/19	Run	9.60	1:10:50	07:22.7	8.1					NXT2
12	3/20	Run	8.50	1:04:25	07:34.7	7.9					NXT2
12	3/21										
12	3/22										
12	3/23	Run	8.20	1:03:31	07:44.8	7.7	8xCB grounds			xa	NXT2
13	3/24	Run	7.60	0:57:15	07:32.0	8.0	2x CB loop			xa	NXT2
13	3/25	Swim	1.79	1:00:41	33:54.3	1.8				xa	
13	3/26	Swim	1.82	1:00:03	33:01.7	1.8				xa	
13	3/27	Run	7.60	0:54:19	07:08.8	8.4	2x CB loop			xa	NXT2
13	3/27	Swim	0.91	0:30:16	33:17.6	1.8				xa	
13	3/28	Run	5.00	2:00:00	24:00.0	2.5	hiking mountains			xa	NXT2
13	3/29	Run	7.60	0:56:29	07:25.9	8.1	2x CB loop			xa	NXT2
13	3/30	Run	26.20	3:13:53	07:24.0	8.1	easy 1:34/1:39				NXT2
14	3/31	Bike	18.50	1:00:00	03:14.6	18.5	CT flat	130	160	x	CT
14	4/1	Swim	1.25	0:39:43	31:46.4	1.9				xa	5S
14	4/2	Run	4.60	0:34:49	07:34.1	7.9	recovery				NXT2
14	4/2	Swim	0.97	0:30:45	31:50.1	1.9				xa	5S
14	4/3	Run	9.10	1:03:30	06:58.7	8.6	BT loop			a	NXT2
14	4/3	Bike	10.00	0:35:13	03:31.3	17.0	10 mile intermediate hills CT	156	226	a	CT
14	4/4	Run	6.90	0:49:30	07:10.4	8.4	hybrid			xa	NXT2
14	4/4	Bike	20.00	0:57:17	02:51.9	20.9	3x6x1.5' 30" RI	145	216	a	CT
14	4/5	Run	4.60	0:33:20	07:14.8	8.3	NT loop			a	NXT2
14	4/5	Swim	0.97	0:31:05	32:10.8	1.9				xa	5S
14	4/6	Run	26.20	3:14:15	07:24.8	8.1	hmx2 1:32/1:42			xa	NXT2
15	4/7	Run	8.70	0:59:34	06:50.8	8.8	BG group rain, wind 38d			xa	BT2
15	4/8	Swim	0.97	0:31:18	32:24.3	1.9				xa	5S
15	4/8	Bike	20.00	0:59:00	02:57.0	20.3	20 mi flat	137	197		CT
15	4/9	Run	9.10	1:03:33	06:59.0	8.6	BT				NXT2
15	4/9	Swim	0.97	0:30:29	31:33.6	1.9	w/Rob			xa	5S
15	4/10	Run	6.10	0:43:57	07:12.3	8.3	AU				BT
15	4/10	Swim	0.94	0:30:17	32:18.1	1.9	AU			xa	
15	4/11	Run	9.10	1:00:15	06:37.3	9.1	BT				NXT2
15	4/12						rest			a	

Week	Date	Type	Dist	Time	Pace	MPH	Exercise	HR	Watts	Wts	Shoes
15	4/13	Run	8.70	0:59:56	06:53.3	8.7	easy; ITB			xa	NXT2
16	4/14						travel to Boston				
16	4/15	Run	26.20	2:54:37	06:39.9	9.0	Boston Marathon				NXT2
16	4/16	Swim	0.91	31:15.7	34:23.3	1.7	recovery			xa	5S
16	4/17	Swim	1.05	34:46.8	33:05.3	1.8	recovery			xas	5S
16	4/18	Swim	0.94	0:30:45	32:48.0	1.8	recovery			xa	5S
16	4/18	Bike	20.40	1:00:00	02:56.5	20.4	CT spin	138	199		CT
16	4/19	Run	9.10	0:59:50	06:34.5	9.1	BT				NXG
16	4/20	Bike	30.75	1:53:00	03:40.5	16.3	easy; wind			xa	SR
17	4/21	Bike	36.20	2:00:00	03:18.9	18.1	IMLP CT	140	186	a	CT
17	4/22	Swim	1.02	0:32:23	31:39.8	1.9				xa	5S
17	4/23	Swim	0.88	0:29:53	33:55.9	1.8	10x100 on 2			xa	5S
17	4/23	Bike	20.00	1:00:00	03:00.0	20.0	CT spin	140	194		CT
17	4/24									xa	
17	4/25	Bike	20.10	1:00:00	02:59.1	20.1	CT NZ	145	198		CT
17	4/26	Swim	0.94	0:30:15	32:16.0	1.9				xa	5S
17	4/27	Bike	39.04	2:10:00	03:19.8	18.0	cool, windy, bonk				SR
18	4/28	Run	9.15	1:00:08	06:34.3	9.1	BG+	162		a	NXG
18	4/29	Swim	1.05	0:32:24	30:49.4	1.9	great			xa	5S
18	4/30	Run	9.10	1:02:54	06:54.7	8.7	BT am				NXG
18	4/30	Swim	0.99	0:31:30	31:40.8	1.9				xa	5S
18	5/1	Bike	10.00	0:37:22	03:44.2	16.1	10 mile intermediate hills CT	150	205		CT
18	5/1	Swim	0.97	0:31:13	32:19.1	1.9				xas	5S
18	5/2	Run	5.27	1:00:00	11:23.1	5.3	P1L8 treadmill	154		a	TM
18	5/3	Run	9.35	1:08:26	07:19.1	8.2	BT+			xa	NXG
18	5/4	Bike	46.80	2:31:00	03:13.6	18.6				a	SR
19	5/5	Bike	20.41	1:08:54	03:22.5	17.8				a	SR
19	5/6	Swim	0.97	0:30:54	31:59.4	1.9				xa	5S
19	5/7	Run	9.10	1:03:37	06:59.5	8.6	BT am	156			NXG
19	5/7	Swim	1.45	0:45:24	31:20.1	1.9				xa	5S
19	5/8	Bike	10.00	0:38:30	03:51.0	15.6	10 mile intermediate hills CT	145		a	CT
19	5/8	Swim	1.90	1:00:05	31:34.0	1.9				x	5S
19	5/9	Run	9.10	1:01:59	06:48.7	8.8	BT			a	NXG
19	5/10	Bike	24.00	1:15:00	03:07.5	19.2	3x8x1.5' CT 60'; 6x Tower hill	155		a	CT
19	5/11	Run	26.20	3:10:21	07:15.9	8.3	2xHM	156			NXG
20	5/13	Bike	10.00	0:37:32	03:45.2	16.0	10 mile intermediate hills CT	150		a	CT
20	5/13	Swim	0.99	0:30:36	30:46.5	1.9	sore ribs			xa	5S
20	5/14	Run	3.95	0:45:00	11:23.5	5.3	P1L8 treadmill	145		a	TM
20	5/14	Swim	1.82	1:00:15	33:08.3	1.8	sore ribs			xa	5S
20	5/15	Bike	101.70	5:10:30	03:03.2	19.7	43m; flat; 58.7m			a	SR
20	5/16	Swim	1.82	1:00:15	33:08.3	1.8	sore ribs			xa	5S
20	5/17	Run	9.10	1:08:13	07:29.8	8.0					NXG
20	5/17	Swim	0.94	0:30:54	32:57.6	1.8	sore ribs			xa	5S
20	5/18	Run	13.10	1:40:00	07:38.0	7.9	rough				NXG
21	5/19	Run	9.10	1:02:37	06:52.9	8.7	BT	159		a	NXG
21	5/22	Run	9.10	1:04:41	07:06.5	8.4				a	NXG
21	5/22	Swim	0.97	0:31:54	33:01.6	1.8	sore ribs			xa	5S
21	5/23	Bike	20.00	0:59:57	02:59.9	20.0	20 mi flat	146	196	a	CT
21	5/24	Run	9.10	0:57:02	06:16.0	9.6	BT			a	NXG
21	5/25	Bike	20.00	0:59:08	02:57.4	20.3	20 mi flat	144	202	a	CT
22	5/26	Run	26.20	2:59:12	06:50.4	8.8	MadCity Marathon				NXG
22	5/27	Run	3.14	0:28:24	09:02.7	6.6	Jubilee Jog 5k with Amanda				NXG
22	5/28	Bike	6.00	0:20:00	03:20.0	18.0	easy spin				CT
22	5/28	Swim	0.65	0:20:09	30:50.3	1.9	AU drills/paddles			xa	
22	5/29	Swim	0.59	0:18:51	31:44.8	1.9					5S
22	5/30	Bike	56.00	2:47:20	02:59.3	20.1	IMNZ lap 1	158	208		CT
22	5/31	Swim	1.00	0:30:35	30:35.0	2.0				xas	5S
22	6/1	Bike	37.25	1:53:30	03:02.8	19.7	GL+			xa	SR
23	6/2	Bike	40.25	2:04:30	03:05.6	19.4	wu some 23 intervals			xa	SR
23	6/3	Bike	23.94	1:14:36	03:07.0	19.3	LF				SR
23	6/3	Swim	0.99	0:31:07	31:17.7	1.9				x	5S
23	6/4	Bike	10.00	0:35:20	03:32.0	17.0	10 mile intermediate hills CT	156	223		CT
23	6/4	Run	2.40	0:25:00	10:25.0	5.8	P1L8 treadmill	156			TM
23	6/4	Swim	1.96	1:01:09	31:11.7	1.9				xa	5S
23	6/5	Swim	0.99	0:29:59	30:09.3	2.0				xa	5S
23	6/6	Run	9.10	1:02:42	06:53.4	8.7	BT			a	NXG
23	6/6	Swim	1.03	0:30:06	29:11.3	2.1	25m pool			s	5S
23	6/7	Bike	23.95	1:11:20	02:58.7	20.1	LF				SR
23	6/7	Swim	1.53	0:46:52	30:36.4	2.0	25m pool			xa	5S
23	6/8	Bike	50.28	2:32:17	03:01.7	19.8					SR
24	6/9	Run	13.10	1:22:54	06:19.7	9.5	North Shore 1/2 Marathon			a	NXG

Week	Date	Type	Dist	Time	Pace	MPH	Exercise	HR	Watts	Wts	Shoes
24	6/10						travel/rest			xa	
24	6/11	Bike	26.90	1:20:00	02:58.4	20.2	LF+V				SR
24	6/11	Swim	1.94	1:01:05	31:31.6	1.9	outside			xa	5S
24	6/12	Bike	28.08	1:24:54	03:01.4	19.8	LF+V			xa	SR
24	6/13	Run	9.40	1:06:56	07:07.2	8.4	BT+				NXG
24	6/14	Bike	26.88	1:17:22	02:52.7	20.8	LF+V				SR
24	6/14	Swim	1.39	0:43:30	31:14.9	1.9	35@30:45+15@12:45 6/12			xa	5S
24	6/15	Bike	50.25	2:30:42	02:59.9	20.0					SR
25	6/16	Run	13.10	1:29:59	06:52.1	8.7	HM				NXG
25	6/18	Run	8.10	1:00:00	07:24.4	8.1	Rochester			xa	NXG1
25	6/19	Run	7.20	0:54:30	07:34.2	7.9	Rochester			xa	NXG1
25	6/20	Bike	26.88	1:16:30	02:50.8	21.1	LF+V	150		a	SR
25	6/21	Bike	26.90	1:16:54	02:51.5	21.0	LF+V	153			SR
25	6/21	Swim	0.66	0:20:29	31:12.8	1.9				xa	5S
25	6/22	Bike	107.60	5:24:00	03:00.7	19.9	Hebron	146			SR
26	6/23	Run	8.70	0:58:35	06:44.0	8.9	BG	162			NXG1
26	6/24	Bike	26.89	1:19:42	02:57.8	20.2	LF+V			a	SR
26	6/24	Swim	1.94	1:00:42	31:19.7	1.9	outside			xa	5S
26	6/25	Bike	16.99	1:08:42	04:02.6	14.8	wu 10x(Tower+Lloyd hills) wd			a	SR
26	6/26	Run	5.27	1:00:00	11:23.1	5.3	P1L8 treadmill				TM
26	6/26	Swim	0.94	0:30:03	32:03.2	1.9	easy outside				5S
26	6/27	Bike	26.90	1:18:16	02:54.6	20.6	LF+V	147			SR
26	6/27	Swim	1.19	0:36:54	31:04.4	1.9	outside			xa	5S
26	6/28	Swim	1.00	0:30:29	30:29.0	2.0	outside			xa	5S
26	6/29	Run	26.20	3:02:59	06:59.0	8.6	first: 1:32:10; second: 1:30:49				NXG
27	6/30	Bike	32.12	1:37:12	03:01.6	19.8	WTB				SR
27	7/1	Bike	26.90	1:16:22	02:50.3	21.1	LF+V				SR
27	7/1	Swim	1.41	0:43:44	31:06.0	1.9				xa	5S
27	7/3	Bike	14.97	0:59:49	03:59.7	15.0	Vwu+10xT+10xL+Vwd				SR
27	7/3	Run	9.55	1:06:41	06:59.0	8.6	BT+				NXG1
27	7/4	Bike	26.90	1:14:34	02:46.3	21.6	LF+V				SR
27	7/4	Run	3.10	0:18:50	06:04.5	9.9	Winnetka 5k brick				NXG1
27	7/5	Bike	101.54	4:59:20	02:56.9	20.4	44+33+24 loops			xa	SR
27	7/6	Run	13.10	1:31:33	06:59.3	8.6	HM	155		xa	NXG
28	7/7	Bike	31.00	1:33:00	03:00.0	20.0	WTB				SR
28	7/8	Bike	27.10	1:19:57	02:57.0	20.3	LFFS+	148		a	SR
28	7/9	Run	9.10	1:04:07	07:02.7	8.5	BT	148		a	NXG1
28	7/9	Swim	1.88	1:00:36	32:19.2	1.9	outside			x	5S
28	7/10	Bike	9.12	0:47:10	05:10.3	11.6	10xTower+10xLloyd hills to L2			a	SR
28	7/10	Swim	1.91	1:00:20	31:39.0	1.9				a	5S
28	7/11	Bike	26.60	1:17:30	02:54.8	20.6	LF+V			a	SR
28	7/11	Run	2.20	0:14:37	06:38.6	9.0	brick				NXG1
28	7/12	Swim	1.03	0:31:57	30:58.9	1.9				xa	5S
28	7/13	Bike	37.93	1:49:00	02:52.4	20.9	brick part 1				SR
28	7/13	Run	13.10	1:30:22	06:53.9	8.7	HM loop brick/ fell on run				NXG1
29	7/14	Run	13.10	1:39:02	07:33.6	7.9	sore shoulder; recovery run	150		a	NXG1
29	7/15	Bike	10.25	0:30:15	02:57.1	20.3					SR
29	7/15	Swim	0.66	0:20:37	31:25.0	1.9	sore shoulder; recovery			x	5S
29	7/16	Run	4.30	0:31:36	07:20.9	8.2	ATL			xa	NXG1
29	7/17	Bike	8.86	0:34:51	03:56.0	15.3	wu 10xTower up to 12mph				SR
29	7/18	Bike	26.80	1:12:38	02:42.6	22.1	Zipps TT				SR
29	7/18	Swim	0.66	0:20:25	31:06.7	1.9					5S
29	7/19	Bike	21.74	1:01:40	02:50.2	21.2	2xGW loop	152		xa	SR
29	7/20	Run	9.10	1:04:30	07:05.3	8.5	sore ribs			a	NXG
30	7/21	Bike	38.00	1:44:00	02:44.2	21.9	brick part 1 Zipp	156			SR
30	7/21	Run	2.20	0:14:49	06:48.6	8.8	brick part 2	156		a	NXG1
30	7/22	Bike	9.90	0:29:40	02:59.8	20.0	spin			a	SR
30	7/23	Run	6.90	0:50:47	07:21.6	8.2	easy				NXG1
30	7/24	Bike	9.90	0:32:10	03:14.9	18.5	nothing				SR
30	7/24	Swim	0.66	0:20:47	31:40.2	1.9	sore shoulder			xa	5S
30	7/26	Bike	12.40	0:42:00	03:23.2	17.7	LP				SR
30	7/27	Swim	0.30	0:12:00	40:00.0	1.5					
30	7/27	Bike	8.00	0:24:00	03:00.0	20.0				a	SR
31	7/28	Swim	2.40	1:10:41	29:27.1	2.0	Ironman USA Lake Placid				
31	7/28	Bike	112.00	5:41:07	03:02.7	19.7	Ironman USA Lake Placid				SR
31	7/28	Run	26.20	3:33:50	08:09.7	7.4	Ironman USA Lake Placid				NXG1
31	7/31	Bike	20.40	1:00:23	02:57.6	20.3	2xGW loop				SR
31	8/1	Bike	21.80	1:05:51	03:01.2	19.9	FS+V				SR

Week	Date	Type	Dist	Time	Pace	MPH	Exercise	HR	Watts	Wts	Shoes
31	8/1	Swim	0.66	0:20:39	31:28.0	1.9	recovery			a	5S
31	8/2	Run	8.60	1:00:35	07:02.7	8.5	recovery	160		xa	NXG
31	8/3	Bike	39.70	1:54:49	02:53.5	20.7	WTB+David	160		xa	SR
32	8/4	Bike	35.30	1:56:44	03:18.4	18.1	w/David	154		a	SR
32	8/4	Swim	0.43	0:15:00	35:12.0	1.7	taping; intervals				5S
32	8/5	Run	4.60	0:32:55	07:09.3	8.4	recovery	154		a	NXG
32	8/5	Swim	0.80	0:25:00	31:25.7	1.9	wu/drills			xa	5S
32	8/6	Swim	0.91	0:30:46	33:50.6	1.8	wu/drills/wd			xa	5S
32	8/7	Bike	14.30	1:01:30	04:18.0	14.0	mixed hill/strength repeats			a	SR
32	8/7	Swim	0.91	0:30:11	33:12.1	1.8	15x50 ~ 46-47 on 60			a	5S
32	8/8	Swim	0.94	0:30:03	32:03.2	1.9	form			a	5S
32	8/9	Run	12.10	1:21:06	06:42.1	9.0	w/BH				NXG1
32	8/10	Bike	37.10	1:55:13	03:06.3	19.3	WTB long wu			a	SR
33	8/11	Run	18.40	2:03:41	06:43.3	8.9	18.2@2:03:41 + 0:01:19	158		a	NXG
33	8/12	Bike	21.80	1:05:11	02:59.4	20.1	FS+V	150			SR
33	8/13	Swim	0.94	0:30:23	32:24.5	1.9	wu/drills/wd			xa	5S
33	8/14	Run	4.60	0:32:30	07:03.9	8.5	NT recoovery	152			NXG
33	8/14	Swim	1.05	0:32:55	31:18.9	1.9				xa	5S
33	8/15	Bike	26.70	1:15:20	02:49.3	21.3	LF+V				SR
33	8/15	Swim	0.97	0:30:07	31:05.3	1.9	outside			xa	5S
33	8/16	Bike	26.70	1:16:11	02:51.2	21.0	LF+V				SR
33	8/17	Run	26.20	3:09:51	07:14.8	8.3	HMX2 1:33/1:36	155		a	NXG
34	8/18	Bike	45.10	2:30:00	03:19.6	18.0	Barrington				SR
34	8/19	Swim	0.91	0:30:04	33:04.8	1.8	wu/drills/wd			xa	5S
34	8/20	Run	8.50	1:07:09	07:54.0	7.6	Glencoe+5xTower Hill	156		a	NXG1
34	8/20	Swim	1.05	0:32:18	30:43.7	2.0	time trial			xa	5S
34	8/21	Bike	21.80	1:01:34	02:49.4	21.2	FS+V			xa	SR
34	8/22	Bike	10.00	0:36:11	03:37.1	16.6	10 mile intermediate hills CT	153	210		CT
34	8/22	Run	1.60	0:15:00	09:22.5	6.4	TM brick	158	1%		TM
34	8/22	Swim	0.99	0:31:03	31:13.6	1.9				xa	5S
34	8/23	Run	9.70	1:08:04	07:01.0	8.6	wu/tempo	147/163			NXG
34	8/23	Swim	0.94	0:30:11	32:11.7	1.9	brick/recovery				5S
34	8/25	Swim	0.94	0:26:45	28:32.0	2.1	Mrs. T's				
34	8/25	Bike	24.80	1:01:15	02:28.2	24.3	Mrs. T's				SR
34	8/25	Run	6.20	0:39:53	06:26.0	9.3	Mrs. T's				NXG1
35	8/26	Swim	1.06	34:06.3	32:05.9	1.9	recovery			xa	5S
35	8/28	Run	5.40	0:41:58	07:46.3	7.7	Boston run			xa	
35	8/30	Run	3.70	0:28:22	07:40.0	7.8	Nantucket			xa	
35	8/31	Run	4.80	0:36:48	07:40.0	7.8	Nantucket			a	
36	9/1	Run	4.10	0:31:44	07:44.4	7.8	Nantucket			a	
36	9/2	Run	4.50	0:34:58	07:46.2	7.7	Nantucket			a	
36	9/4	Bike	10.00	0:38:50	03:53.0	15.5	10 mile intermediate hills CT	164	179		CT
36	9/4	Swim	0.91	0:30:30	33:33.0	1.8	TI drills			xa	5S
36	9/5	Bike	20.00	1:00:00	03:00.0	20.0	Kona first 20	L3	214		CT
36	9/5	Swim	0.94	0:30:30	32:32.0	1.8	easy TI			xa	5S
36	9/6	Swim	1.05	0:33:12	31:35.1	1.9	TI			xn	5S
36	9/7	Bike	39.00	2:00:55	03:06.0	19.4	WTB			a	SR
37	9/8	Run	13.10	1:26:09	06:34.6	9.1	HM loop			xa	NXG1
37	9/9	Bike	15.40	0:46:17	03:00.3	20.0	spin			a	SR
37	9/9	Swim	0.63	0:19:53	31:48.8	1.9	easy				CT
37	9/10	Run	8.50	1:01:53	07:16.8	8.2	easy				NXG1
37	9/11	Run	11.80	0:34:03	02:53.1	20.8					SR
37	9/12	Swim	0.65	0:20:00	30:36.5	2.0	drills			xan	5S
37	9/13	Bike	5.70	0:20:00	03:30.5	17.1	test				SR
38	9/15	Swim	2.40	1:15:29	31:27.1	1.9	Ironman Wisconsin				
38	9/15	Bike	112.00	5:37:58	03:01.1	19.9	Ironman Wisconsin				SR
38	9/15	Run	26.20	3:36:16	08:15.3	7.3	Ironman Wisconsin				NXG1
38	9/17	Swim	0.45	0:15:04	33:08.8	1.8	recovery			xa	5S
38	9/18	Swim	0.48	0:15:29	32:03.6	1.9	recovery			xa	5S
38	9/20	Swim	0.68	0:21:37	31:42.3	1.9	recovery				5S
38	9/21	Bike	30.60	1:36:17	03:08.8	19.1	WTB			xa	SR
39	9/22	Run	6.30	0:47:29	07:32.2	8.0	recovery			xa	NXG1
39	9/23	Bike	19.25	1:00:30	03:08.6	19.1	Kona first 20	150	214		CT
39	9/24	Swim	1.05	0:33:27	31:49.4	1.9				xa	5S
39	9/25	Bike	25.00	1:10:48	02:49.9	21.2	3x8x2.5%2%0watts RI 30" 10'w/u	L3	232	a	CT
39	9/26	Swim	1.88	1:00:03	32:01.6	1.9				a	5S

Week	Date	Type	Dist	Time	Pace	MPH	Exercise	HR	Watts	Wts	Shoes
39	9/27	Run	9.10	1:06:19	07:17.3	8.2	BT			a	NXG1
39	9/28	Run	10.90	1:21:57	07:31.1	8.0	JP hill route			a	NXG1
40	9/29	Bike	29.10	1:30:00	03:05.6	19.4	Kona first 29	150	205	a	CT
40	9/30	Swim	0.48	0:15:10	31:24.2	1.9				xa	5S
40	9/30	Bike	18.20	1:00:00	03:17.8	18.2	Kona first 18	150	181	a	CT
40	10/1	Bike	27.20	1:46:23	03:54.7	15.3	Kona 30 to Hawi w/hdwind	150	193		CT
40	10/1	Run	1.60	0:15:00	09:22.5	6.4	brick after CT	150	1%	a	TM
40	10/2	Bike	13.00	0:42:32	03:16.3	18.3	10'wu + PR 10mlint 32:32	168	257	a	CT
40	10/2	Run	2.80	0:24:00	08:34.3	7.0	brick after CT	160	1%	xa	TM
40	10/3	Run	8.60	1:00:33	07:02.4	8.5	LT			a	NXG
40	10/5	Bike	27.00	1:28:00	03:15.6	18.4	WTB			a	SR
41	10/6	Run	6.20	0:39:01	06:17.6	9.5	Winnetka 10k			a	NXG1
41	10/9	Swim	1.88	1:01:20	32:42.7	1.8				xa	5S
41	10/9	Run	9.10	0:57:15	06:17.5	9.5	BT				NXG2
41	10/10	Bike	60.30	3:01:48	03:00.9	19.9	(GL+V) + (LF+V)				SR
41	10/12	Run	3.50	0:26:22	07:32.0	8.0	easy				NXG
42	10/13	Run	26.20	3:05:32	07:04.9	8.5	Chicago Marathon				NXG1
42	10/14	Swim	0.45	0:14:44	32:24.8	1.9	recovery			xa	5S
42	10/19	Swim	2.40	1:18:57	32:53.8	1.8	Ironman Hawaii				
42	10/19	Bike	112.00	6:01:54	03:13.9	18.6	Ironman Hawaii				SR
42	10/19	Run	26.20	3:50:14	08:47.3	6.8	Ironman Hawaii				NXG2
43	10/26	Run	6.00	0:45:32	07:35.3	7.9	recovery			xa	NXG2
44	10/27	Bike	9.00	0:30:00	03:20.0	18.0	CT spin		140	xa	CT
44	10/29	Swim	0.82	0:25:46	31:16.5	1.9	recovery			xa	5S
44	10/30	Swim	0.80	0:25:36	32:11.0	1.9	recovery			xa	5S
44	11/2	Run	3.60	0:27:08	07:32.2	8.0	recovery			xa	NXG2
45	11/4	Swim	0.91	0:28:47	31:39.7	1.9	recovery			xa	5S
45	11/8	Swim	0.91	0:28:53	31:46.3	1.9	recovery			x	5S
45	11/9	Run	8.50	1:06:01	07:46.0	7.7	Jog/walk with Eric/Kirsten			xa	NXG2
46	11/10	Run	8.70	1:02:16	07:09.4	8.4	pushing Kirsten in baby jogger			a	NXG2
46	11/12	Bike	10.00	0:36:25	03:38.5	16.5	10 mile intermediate hills CT	L2	210	xa	CT
46	11/12	Run	2.00	0:24:00	12:00.0	5.0	P1L7 hill TM brick	158		xa	TM
46	11/13	Bike	20.00	0:56:11	02:48.6	21.4	Twenty mile flat DT 95 cadence	Z2 Z3	227	xa	CT
46	11/14	Run	5.27	1:00:00	11:23.1	5.3	P1L8 treadmill hills	Run Z1		xa	TM
46	11/16	Run	8.60	1:05:32	07:37.2	7.9				a	NXG1
47	11/18	Bike	20.00	0:58:36	02:55.8	20.5	Twenty mile flat CT 90 cadence	Z3-L1	210	xa	CT
47	11/19	Swim	0.94	0:29:44	31:42.9	1.9				xa	5S
47	11/20	Run	9.10	1:00:46	06:40.7	9.0	BT			xa	NXG2
47	11/21	Bike	25.00	1:10:00	02:48.0	21.4	Twenty-five mile flat CT 90-95	L1-L3	230	a	CT
48	11/24	Bike	25.00	1:10:00	02:48.0	21.4	Twenty-five mile flat CT 90-95	L2-L3	230	a	CT
48	11/25	Run	3.50	0:31:00	08:51.4	6.8	TM various	144		xa	TM
48	11/26	Bike	21.80	1:05:00	02:58.9	20.1	CT IMNZ various	Z3-L1	220	xa	CT
48	11/27	Run	8.60	1:06:44	07:45.6	7.7	easy run in snow			xa	NXG2
48	11/28	Run	8.60	1:04:05	07:27.1	8.1	NL Loop: 20 degrees			xa	NXG2
48	11/29	Run	6.20	0:47:24	07:38.7	7.8				xa	NXG2
48	11/30	Run	13.40	1:44:29	07:47.8	7.7	HM+beach+: cold, windy			xa	NXG2
49	12/1	Bike	22.00	1:04:20	02:55.5	20.5	CT flat	Z2-Z3	213	xa	CT
49	12/2	Run	5.75	1:00:00	10:26.1	5.8	TM 45' P1L7 + 15' 1% 7.7	Run 2 6%-1		xa	TM
49	12/4	Bike	19.00	1:00:00	03:09.5	19.0	10' wu + 50' Kona CT	Z3	213	xa	CT
49	12/5	Swim	0.88	0:28:42	32:35.3	1.8					5S
49	12/6	Swim	0.94	0:29:18	31:15.2	1.9	better			xa	5S
49	12/7	Run	7.80	0:56:57	07:18.1	8.2	SG Gillson				NXG1
50	12/8	Bike	16.80	1:00:00	03:34.3	16.8	CDTO CT course	Z3-L1	209	a	CT
50	12/9	Run	5.27	1:00:00	11:23.1	5.3	P1L8 TM hill course	Run Z2		a	TM
50	12/10	Bike	15.00	0:50:30	03:22.0	17.8	10'wu+45'intercal+5'mintintercal CT	Z3-L3	230	a	CT
50	12/11	Swim	1.85	1:00:35	32:48.5	1.8	easy			x	5S
50	12/12	Swim	1.88	1:00:34	32:18.1	1.9				x	5S
50	12/13	Run	6.20	0:47:41	07:41.5	7.8	LT am			a	NXG3
50	12/14	Run	12.50	1:29:28	07:09.4	8.4	BSL 6@3"; 3 in ice; late hills			a	NXG3
51	12/15	Run	10.00	1:15:58	07:35.8	7.9	BH+ to/from HP			a	NXG3
51	12/16	Bike	20.00	1:00:30	03:01.5	19.8	spin	Z1-Z2			CT
51	12/18	Bike	21.44	1:00:00	02:47.9	21.4	3x6x1.5' RI 30" 2'RI	L1-L3	230	a	CT
51	12/19	Run	3.90	0:25:30	06:32.3	9.2	crash at Gillson				NXG3
52	12/25	Bike	20.20	1:00:00	02:58.2	20.2	CT flat recovery ride	Z3-L1	205	xa	CT
52	12/26	Run	9.10	1:11:49	07:53.5	7.6	BT half snow/recovery easy			a	NXG1
52	12/27	Run	9.10	1:11:29	07:51.3	7.6	BT 15 degrees; snow; bone	170+		a	NXG
52	12/27	Bike	26.20	1:15:00	02:51.8	21.0	IMNZ 26.2 of lap 1	L1-L3	223	a	CT
52	12/28	Run	9.10	1:05:30	07:11.9	8.3	BT loop -- better!	165ish			NXG2
52	12/28	Bike	28.00	1:18:49	02:48.9	21.3	IMNZ 28 of lap 1	L1-L2	225	a	CT
53	12/29	Run	9.10	1:03:50	07:00.9	8.6	BT	165			NXG2
53	12/30	Run	13.10	1:31:23	06:58.5	8.6	HM	162			NXG2
53	12/31	Run	13.10	1:33:57	07:10.3	8.4	HM sore knee	162			NXG2

Everything Else You Need To Know

At each Ironman race these days – or Half Ironman, Olympic Distance, or even Sprint races for that matter – hundreds or more of the athletes are tackling triathlon for the first time.

And they all have the same questions: What do I need to take? What do I do when I get there? What should I expect? What do I need to carry? What might go wrong? How do I deal with it?

It can seem overwhelming. So much to do, so much to remember.

Let me simplify it for you.

Do what you or your coach think is right to get you to the point where you're ready to race, ready to cover the distance. I'll help you with the rest – what to expect and what to do – from packing for your trip to crossing the finish line:

- What to Take
- Assembly Once You Get There
- Bike Check-in
- Planning Nutrition
- Race Morning – Final Preparations
- The Race: Swim, Transition, Bike, Transition, Run
- Finishing With a Smile

It takes a few races to get it all figured out, believe me. With 29 Ironman finishes over the last nine years, I think I can pretty well answer many of those questions for rookies, and even for those that have done more than one race, but are still looking for the right combination.

What to Take

There are so many things to pack or, put another way, so many things to potentially forget. And yes, I have forgotten many different things over the years.

But I have learned not to panic, for a simple reason: even if you forgot <u>everything</u>, you still could buy just about all of it
at the race merchandise area. Just knowing you have that backstop should make your packing less worrisome.

Because I'll tell you right now: you will forget something, probably a few somethings. Don't worry. Wetsuits, Bikes, components, nutrition, just about everything but running shoes (which you can buy at a sporting goods store) can typically be found on site.

But to remember to bring the right things, here's the approach: pre-pack your transition bags.

Create five piles in the packing room, one each for Prerace, Swim, Bike, Run, Nutrition. As you grab items from your closet, bags, car, wherever, lay them in the appropriate piles.

My basics are:

- Prerace: clothes to wear to/from transition – jacket and sweatpants, and what I'll wear during the entire race – bike shirt, tri-shorts, timing chip and strap
- Swim: wetsuit, goggles, sunscreen, body glide, extra swim cap, swimsuit
- Bike: helmet, sunglasses, bike shoes, gloves, race belt, socks, arm warmers
- Run: hat, shoes, extra race belt, socks, and sunglasses if you need them
- Nutrition/other: bring the essentials you are sure you won't find on the race site. A favorite gel, certain salt tablets or pain reliever, perhaps. Have a small plastic container – I prefer a 35mm film holder – to hold salt and ibuprofen on the bike.

Place the contents into five bags, labeled accordingly, and drop them in your suitcase. For me, one of those bags is an athletic bag, which I later use to carry things to/from transition.

Packing the bike can be intimidating. After dialing in your perfect position, the last thing you want to do is disassemble it. To restore your bike to that perfect position later, use black electrical tape to mark measurements. Seat post, handlebars, anything that moves or is removed should have a tape mark. Do that, and you can return to your perfect dialed-in position when you reassemble your bike.

So you're not scrambling on race day, pack your saddle bag in advance with everything you'll need before the trip. Replacement tube or tire, glue if necessary, co2 adapter (buy co2 on site), disc wheel air adapter (if necessary), hex tool, extra contact lenses (yes, you might need them).

Pressing bike pieces inside a tight transport case is a scary concept. To avoid friction in transit, wrap the frame and anything else that might have contact in bubble wrap or some other protective material. I use several Velcro straps use to secure the protection in place. And knowing how bike cases can be tossed around behind airline counters, I've added Velcro on the outside of the case itself to further secure the contents.

Follow these steps, and you should have just about everything you need with you when you arrive at the race registration.

Assembly

Unpack soon after arriving to make sure you brought everything, or more important, to find out if you forgot anything. Time flies surprisingly fast once you get to the race city, and if you need something – I usually do, CO_2 cartridges and GU at a minimum – you need to find out early.

It's especially important to get your bike assembled and tested right away. If a screw gets stripped or a tire won't inflate, you want to know that as soon as possible. There's nothing worse than finding out your bike stem needs to be replaced right before bike check-in, and then scrambling to find the right size, shape, whatever. Yes, it's happened to me, and yes, I've panicked when the right part couldn't be found. You don't want that to happen to you.

After you get your race transition bags at registration, lay them out, and match the Swim, Bike, Run bags you had packed earlier. It's as simple as transferring the contents – you've already pre-packed your transition bags. Again, if you forgot anything, you'll find out at this time, and have the opportunity to buy what's missing.

An important note about bib numbers and race belts. Bib numbers can be flimsy, can tear, and can fly off during the race. And losing your number can mean a penalty (silly rule, but I've seen it enforced). My secret to avoiding all this: black electrical tape. Put black electrical tape over the top two holes of your bib number, front and back. This more than doubles the reinforcement. Then poke the pin on your race belt through the electrical tape to secure the bib number. The electrical tape holds perfectly. I've never lost a bib number on the course with this method.

xBike Check-In

In my early races, I remember being particularly worried that I'd forgotten something essential on the day of bike and transition bag check-in the day before the race. I'd check and recheck the bags, and still be nervous.

But there's no reason for concern. At most races, you have access to your bags race morning, and if you forget anything, you can add it then. Again, relax.

Just make sure you've got the basics in the bags: bib number, helmet, bike shoes, running shoes. If you swim in your tri-outfit, you can finish the race with just those items. Everything else – sunglasses, gloves, socks, hat – extra. If you have it there, perfect. If you forgot, don't sweat it.

It's pretty easy to find bikes belonging to some of the triathlon rookies at any race. How to spot them? Easy. Three water bottles already in cages on the bike, and nutrition already put in place. PowerBar squares sticking to the top tube of some bikes, an open invitation for bugs. Nasty.

Believe me, after exposure to a hot day and a cool night, that stuff will not be appealing on race day. Keep your nutrition and bottles with you overnight, and put them in place on race morning.

I had a string of triathlons that involved rain the night before the race, and now bring plastic trash bags to put over handlebars and the seat if the forecast suggests a wet night. Covering the handlebars means a dry surface to tape nutrition (all my GU slipped off wet handlebars in transition at one race). Some people cover their chain, too. Some cover the entire bike. That's overkill for me, but it's up to you.

After that, you'll have nothing to do except relax and think about the nutrition and hydration you'll carry the following day.

Planning Race Nutrition

Planning your hydration and nutrition needs for an Ironman can be tricky. Too much and you'll feel sick, too little and you'll bonk. And then there's the worry about how to get enough calories during the day. I've seen sandwiches strapped to handlebars. I've ridden with riders whose watches beeped every fifteen minutes telling them to eat more fig bars. I've seen athletes load up a Camelback to carry fluid with them on the bike and the same athletes stop in their tracks at Special Needs to reload another bladder of fluid.

It all seems like so much work. It has to be simpler.

It took me many races of trial and error to find the right mix. What I ended up with may be a formula that can be applied to your needs, though the specific ingredients might change.

After many races, I found that about about 2500 to 3000 calories was my optimal calorie count on the bike. Simply, that translates to about 250 calories every 10 miles on the bike. This amount not only keeps me fueled for the bike, but also prepares me for the run. So that is my target. Practice caloric intake on your long training rides to find the level right for you.

In terms of how to get those calories, here's what I came up with:

- 800 calories GU: 8 packets, 100 calories each, Plain is the preferred flavor
- 920 calories PowerBars: 4 chocolate PowerBars,
- 300 calories: Bananas: grab 6 bananas at aid stations
- 750 calories Gatorade: take at least 5 bottles Gatorade, one every other aid station, 5 x 125 calories

Race Morning: Final Preparations

My race morning routine is simple.

First, you can arrive terrifyingly early. Don't. As long as you can get there an hour before the race, you're fine. Arrive two hours early, and you've added anxiety time. Relax.

Second, get the bike ready:

- Tape the 8 GU gels to aerobars, four on each side
- Place four PowerBars in Profile-Design Velcro pouch on the top of my Softride beam
- Put the plastic container (35mm film) container with ibuprofen and sodium in the pouch
- Insert one water bottle in bottle cage (with regular aid stations, I see no reason to carry more)
- Check the tires
- Put White Lightning on the chain
- Set the bike computer distance and time setting to zero

Next, I go to transition area and make sure at least helmet, bike shoes, bib number and running shoes are in the bags. That's the minimum you need, if you forgot anything.

After that. Relax, breathe deep, and look forward to a fun day of endurance. Now all you have to do is travel 140.6 miles (or the distance of your triathlon). Again, don't worry. Plenty of time -- you've got 17 hours to do it.

Swim

In my experience, not too much can go terribly wrong in the swim. You get through it, either quickly, or not. How fast you go depends on your training.

How much physical contact you endure depends on where you start. I've tried starting everywhere: at the rear, up front, inside on the 'line', outside. There will be contact no matter where you start.

Someone will inadvertently kick you. You will accidentally bump into someone else. It may feel violent, but no one wants to hurt anyone. Do not take it personally. Know that the person who almost knocked your goggles off really wished that didn't happen, sorry. Relax.

If you start at the rear and you're willing to wait about 30 seconds after the cannon goes off, it can be a fairly breezy swim. The benefit is a complete draft of all swimmers in front of you; the downside may be that you need to navigate around many people.

Most of the time, I hope to start on the side, near the front, with the hope that it will not be congested. Except that hundreds of athletes also seem to have the same idea. So the sides tend to be pretty densely packed.

For the rookie who's not an expert swimmer, relax at the swim start, let others start ahead of you, and do your best to swim in a straight line. If you lose five or ten minutes on a slow swim, you can make it up on the bike or run.

For the rookies who are fast swimmers, I envy you. Go to the front, swim well, and enjoy being in front of most of the athletes for a while. Say hi to me when I pass you on the bike.

Swim to Bike Transition

I am usually disoriented coming out of the water. It's not easy to immediately adjust to land after more than an hour bobbing and weaving through the water. Take your time exiting the water, and begin running to transition. Volunteers may be there to help remove your wetsuit. After that, other volunteers will help you find your transition bag. Thank them for helping you.

Find a seat, put on your helmet, bib number, socks and shoes. Make sure debris is off your feet first, because you may choose to run in those socks later. Decide if you want to take arm warmers. My advice: when in doubt, be comfortable. I usually wear arm warmers on the bike, knowing I might discard them later. And I'm usually glad I have them.

Get sunscreen before you head out to get your bike. Volunteers will slather it on you in fifteen seconds. Skip that step, and you will be explaining strange sunburn patterns to your family later.

Bike

For me, the first few hours on the bike are perhaps the most enjoyable part of the Ironman. You feel fresh, you feel fast, people are in good moods. And then there's the scenery. Every course has wonderful scenery, in its own way. It's one of the reasons we race.

Can something go wrong on your bike ride, the one you prepared so diligently for? Sure. Be prepared for it, not afraid.

Something different seems to happen to me in every race. I've had flat tires in Austria and in the US. I've had contact lenses fly out of my eyes on the bike in Canada and in Germany. More than once I've pulled my bike out of transition, only to see 1000 calories of nutrition fly off the bike onto the street (I've learned a thing or two about securing nutrition in place as a result).

The point is, expect the unexpected, and embrace it as part of the triathlon experience. Being a triathlete is about overcoming obstacles. Unexpected problems included.

I saw several people on the side of the road on the Ironman Arizona 2006 bike course with flat tires or some other bike mechanical problem. More than a few of them had looks of deep despair, head in hands. They were looks of shattered dreams. And at the moment, they may have been. But there are other chances, other races. I've done enough races to know that a single race is never the definitive one. Do what you can to get back on the course, and finish.

If you get a flat tire, try to change it. I flew all the way to Austria, in hope of a fast race in 2001, only to flat on the first loop. I lost 10 minutes changing the flat, and that wasn't too bad. I didn't let it kill my day.

In Ironman USA Lake Placid 2005, two of the three screws on my cycling shoe cleat fell out. I stropped to try to fix it to no avail, then rode the last 25 miles gingerly with a loose cleat. It cost me many precious minutes (and I missed a Kona slot by one minute), but I've decided life is too short to worry about things that happen. They do. You'll be fine.

If you need to wait for race support for help, it could take a long time. If that happens, don't get upset, just change your goal. A friend waited 45 minutes waiting for assistance at Ironman Idaho, after which he found himself almost completely at the rear of all athletes. So he changed the challenge. He would now try to see how many people he could pass for the remainder of the bike ride. He must have passed more than 1000 people, and was satisfied with that.

Executing the bike nutrition plan is about as simple as putting it together. Remember, your exact nutrition may vary, but the concept is the same – balanced calorie input throughout your ride. Here's the timing. Simple.

- GU: Take a GU sometime within every 10 mile segment. That gets you to 80 miles. Easy to remember, each time you see a mile marker with a zero, eat a GU.
- PowerBar: Eat a PowerBar within every 25 mile segment. Yes, this overlaps with GU somewhat, but that's not a problem. I usually eat them between miles 15 and 20, 40 and 45, and 65 and 70. The last one depends on how I'm feeling late in the ride.
- Gatorade: it's essential to always have one with you on the bike. Grab one each aid station and put it in a bottle cage.
- Water: I also grab a water bottle, but try to swig half of it then toss it by the end of the aid station. With aid stations every 10 miles, I can't come up with a reason to carry more than one bottle.
- Bananas: it's unpredictable which aid stations will have them, so I grab one each time I see it. Some races do not have bananas, and you might have to substitute. Just make sure you grab those 300 calories somewhere.
- Salt/Ibuprofen: I took a salt tablet and an ibuprofen tablet every 30 miles. Read directions to make sure your ibuprofen dose is appropriate.

I don't use special needs bags on the bike or run. I decided long ago it's not worth the hassle. Everything I need is on the bike or at aid stations. I think the same is true for most athletes. Not to mention my experience is that getting your bag in a timely manner tends to be a challenge, and most of the time what you included in the bag is not appealing when you actually get it.

Bike To Run Transition

By the time you finish the bike, you're feeling ready to run. At least mentally. Ready to run in the sense that you're ready to not ride anymore, at a minimum.

Reality will set in when you hop off the bike, give it to a waiting volunteer, and begin to head towards transition. Those first few steps after 112 miles are quite a surprise. You feel like you almost can't move forward. Your first thought may be: I don't think I can 26.2 miles now.

Rest assured that in about 30 seconds, you'll feel better. Keep running, pick up your bag, and get to the change tent. By the time you get your running shoes and hat on, you'll feel surprisingly ready to run. Get more sunscreen, acknowledge the cheers of the spectators on the railing, and head out onto the run course.

Run

In the same way you might get a flat tire on the run, you may physically flat on the run. Cramps, bad patches, tough times. For the Ironman rookie, this might be the longest continuous timeframe you've ever moved your body forward. It may want to give out soon. But know that sometimes it can get better after it gets worse. Keep moving forward, keep hydrating and drinking.

Most aid stations, usually only one mile apart, have water, cola, Gatorade, chicken broth, oranges, bananas, pretzels, GU and ice. Train with these, and you'll need nothing more on race day.

The run hydration/nutrition plan is even simpler than on the bike, because you don't need to carry anything. I've worked out similar 'rules' for consistency, including:

- Two cups of cola with ice at least every other aid station. Cola provides sugar, caffeine and sodium. That's about 50 calories x 13 = 650 calories
- If bearable, GU every 4 miles. That's about 600 calories if you get them all.
- When the chicken broth is available, take it. It's Go Juice. High levels of sodium will make you feel better, guaranteed. Though the mix of cola and broth in your stomach might not feel the best.

At Ironman Arizona, because of the very dry air, I found myself needing to have cola at every aid station. Do what you need to do. The only thing to avoid is getting behind on your hydration or nutrition. Try to keep up.

And run as the best you can, at least at a pace that you can sustain for a few hours. If you need to walk a hill or two, do it. Walk the aid stations. Keep moving forward. Nothing will keep you from your Ironman finish. It's just a matter of time now.

Finish

You've trained all year to get there. You've raced all day to get there. Enjoy the moments in the final meters of the finish line chute. Let others enjoy their moment, too. Don't race someone to the finish line, unless you think a Kona slot is on the line. Let the racer in front of you get a finish line photo to cherish. Then go get your own.

Cross the line, smile for the camera, and consider yourself a member of the club. You are an Ironman.

Finish Line

I hope this Book provides the information you need to have a great Ironman race. If there are some questions that still need answers, feel free to contact me via my website, www.RunTri.com.

There is no experience like racing and finishing the Ironman Triathlon. But the experience getting there can be every bit as rewarding, too.

Good luck in your quest for your best Ironman race. There is no experience like racing and finishing the Ironman Triathlon. But the experience getting there can be every bit as rewarding, too. Enjoy every minute.

About the Author

Raymond Britt is Managing Partner at WinSight Ventures, publisher of RunTri.com and one of the most experienced endurance athletes in the world.

Few can match Britt's extensive competitive record. He's completed 29 Ironman Triathlons (2.4 mile swim, 112 mile bike ride, 26.2 mile run), 48 Marathons, 8 Ultramarathons (31 or more miles) and more than 60 other triathlons and running races.

Since his debut race – the 1994 Chicago Marathon – Britt has covered nearly 50,000 training and racing miles around the globe. He's finished the Chicago Marathon 12 times, the Boston Marathon 13 consecutive times, Hawaii Ironman World Championships 3 times, and has been a USA Triathlon All-American.

Britt's articles, photographs and perspectives have been featured by CNN, NBC, New York Times, USA Today, Chicago Tribune, Chicago Sun-Times, Los Angeles Times, Triathlete magazine, Running Times magazine and many others.

As publisher of RunTri.com, Britt serves an annual audience of 500,000 worldwide readers, providing free training and racing resources to help athletes achieve their goals.

Made in the USA
Lexington, KY
25 September 2010